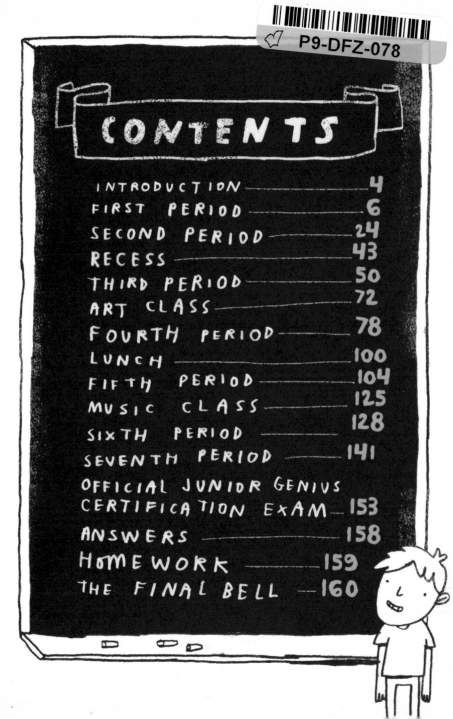

CONTENTS

INTRODUCTION —————— 4
FIRST PERIOD —————— 6
SECOND PERIOD ———— 24
RECESS ——————— 43
THIRD PERIOD———— 50
ART CLASS———— 72
FOURTH PERIOD——— 78
LUNCH ———————— 100
FIFTH PERIOD———— 104
MUSIC CLASS———— 125
SIXTH PERIOD ———— 128
SEVENTH PERIOD —— 141
OFFICIAL JUNIOR GENIUS
CERTIFICATION EXAM— 153
ANSWERS ————— 158
HOMEWORK ——— 159
THE FINAL BELL —160

INTRODUCTION

Em hotep nefer! That, my friends, is a greeting that means "In beautiful peace." But you probably didn't understand me, because I was using a language that hasn't been heard on earth for centuries!

I'm Professor Jennings, and today we're going to travel back in time to the Nile River Valley five thousand years ago and learn about life in one of  history's greatest civilizations: ancient Egypt! While most of the world was still living in caves and huts, the Egyptians were inventing geometry, writing, and toothpaste, not to mention building stone monuments fifty stories high.

How did they do it? What were their lives like? Where did they go?

I'm glad you are asking questions like this, because the official Junior Genius motto is *"Semper quaerens"*— "Always curious." Let's begin by saying the Junior Genius Pledge! Place your right finger to your temple, face this drawing of Albert Einstein, and repeat after me!

With all my fellow Junior Geniuses, I solemnly pledge to quest after questions, to angle for answers, to seek out, and to soak up. I will hunger and thirst for knowledge my whole life through, and I dedicate my discoveries to all humankind, with trivia not for just us but for all.

THIS MAY LOOK LIKE A SMALL HANDHELD BOOK, BUT IT'S ACTUALLY A TIME MACHINE. WHEN YOU TURN THIS PAGE, YOU WILL BE MORE THAN FIVE THOUSAND YEARS IN THE PAST.

READY?...SET...*TURN!*

FIRST PERIOD

THE BLACK LAND

. . . And now we're in the year 3500 BC, the very end of the Stone Age. Here are some things that haven't been invented yet:

Bronze
Written language
The wheel

The world population is less than fifteen million. In our time that's about the population of the Los Angeles area. But here in 3500 BC, that's every single human being *on earth*.

The fall of Troy is more than two thousand years in the future. The Vikings are more than *four* thousand

years away. It goes without saying that your parents and teachers haven't been born yet, so don't bother doing your homework tonight.

DRY, DRY AGAIN

Let's say that we've traveled in space as well as time. We're now in Africa, in the hottest desert on earth—the Sahara.

But the Sahara wasn't always a desert. If we traveled back in time five thousand more years, we'd find a very different Sahara.

Back then the Sahara was a grassy savannah. There was plenty of rain, thanks to (monsoon) winds from the *Look it up!* Mediterranean and melting glaciers from the previous ice age.

THE SAHARA

THEN

NOW

7

But around 4000 BC, that all changed. The rains stopped, the grass died, lakes and rivers dried up. Once the grasses were gone, the soil blew away, leaving only baked sand underneath.

Pretty much everyone left or died.

DELTA FORCE

But our story doesn't end there, or this would be the worst time-travel trip *ever*!

It's time to meet the main character in our story, the one who made Egyptian civilization happen. This character isn't a priest or a pharaoh or one of those gods with the weird animal heads. It's a river.

The Nile River is one of the longest rivers in the world. It runs more than half the length of Africa, from high in the mountains of Rwanda down to the Mediterranean Sea. That's more than 4,000 miles, longer than the border between the contiguous United States and Canada.

EXTRA CREDIT

The Nile was long believed to be the world's longest river, but in 2001 a group of National Geographic explorers climbed an extinct volcano in the Andes mountains of South America and discovered a new source for the Amazon River. It now looks like the Amazon might be a *teensy* bit longer than the Nile— by a hundred miles or fewer.

During the last one hundred miles of the Nile's journey to the sea, it spreads out into a web of smaller rivers that drain into the Mediterranean. Areas like this are often triangular in shape, like the Greek letter delta,

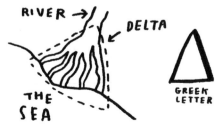

so they're called river deltas.

When the Sahara was nice and green, the Nile delta was a

terrible swamp that everyone stayed away from. But as the desert dried out, nomadic hunters migrated down to the river to find game. The Nile valley turned into a pretty great place to live.

Well, maybe "pretty great" is overstating things a bit. The Egyptian desert certainly has its good points and its bad points.

BAD POINTS

The sand is crawling with venomous scorpions and snakes.

Blisteringly hot winds called *khamsin* blow in from the south every spring, causing sandstorms.

In the fall, locusts buzz in to eat your crops—but you get only about an inch of rain every year, so you might not have crops anyway.

The river is full of deadly hippos and crocodiles.

GOOD POINTS

The Nile rises twenty-three feet every summer, flooding the valley.

That's right: Life in Egypt is so hard that an annual flood is as good as it gets!

Let me explain.

A RIVER FLOODS THROUGH IT

When the Nile flooded every June, it left behind a layer of black dirt called *silt*. Date palms and fig trees grew in this fertile soil. Farmers could plant wheat and barley there. The early Egyptians called their valley *Kemet*, meaning "the black land." The black land was only a mile wide in some places. Everything beyond was endless sand—*Deshret*, "the red land."

BLACK IS BEAUTIFUL

Because of the color of Kemet's fertile soil, black was the color of good luck in Egypt. Many of the statues of gods we've found in Egyptian tombs are painted with black resin. The color red was the opposite: It meant trouble. On an Egyptian calendar red symbols meant something bad had happened on that day—or was about to.

These floods were the only thing that made life in ancient Egypt possible. For the Egyptians, each year had three seasons:

AKHET (FLOOD)   PERET (GROWTH)   SHEMU (HARVEST)

The Egyptians didn't know the Nile's rise was because of snow melting in the mountains of southern Africa. In fact, they'd never even heard of snow. They thought the floods were caused by a goddess crying.

About once every five years, the Nile didn't deposit enough silt, and there would be a famine. Egypt's priests were in charge of assuring a good summer flood, and they took the job seriously. They learned that the appearance of the star Sirius in the sky just before dawn meant that flood season was beginning. They also invented measuring sticks called *nilometers* to predict the strength of the flood.

So the flooding helped Egypt develop science.

Some years the flood would be so strong that it would wash away fields and villages. Towns had to band together to build dikes that would keep back the Nile, as well as canals to manage and share the irrigation water. So the flooding helped unite Egypt as well.

TOO MUCH FLOODING

JUST RIGHT

EXTRA CREDIT

In the 1960s Egypt spent $1 billion to build the Aswan High Dam, a massive two-mile-long wall of dirt and rocks across the Nile River. The dam produces electricity and helps prevent drought. But it also means that, after thousands of years, the annual flooding of the Nile River has finally ended.

UP IS DOWN

The Nile River, like the vast Sahara desert, helped keep Egypt isolated from the rest of the Middle East. Head downstream toward the delta, and you'd reach impassable marshes.

NOT ENOUGH

Head upstream, and you'd hit waterfalls and rapids. As a result, throughout their history the Egyptians mostly kept to themselves. That's one reason their culture was so amazing and unique.

But in the beginning there wasn't one Egypt. There were two.

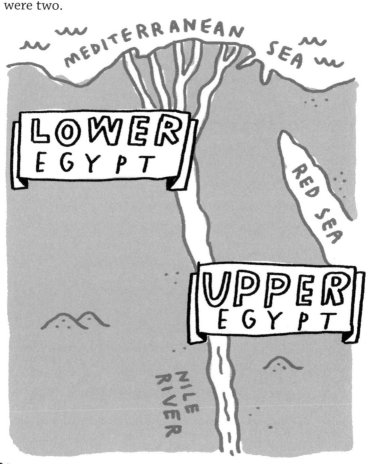

Does it bother you that Lower Egypt is upper and Upper Egypt is lower? If so, please turn this book upside down.

The names refer to *altitude*, my friends. Upper Egypt is uphill; Lower Egypt is closer to sea level. But many Egyptian mapmakers did orient their charts with south at the top of the page, the opposite of what we do today. It was just common sense in Egypt: The river flows down, so we'll put north at the bottom of the page. In fact, when an Egyptian army invaded Syria in 1525 BC, the soldiers *freaked out* when they realized some rivers in other countries flowed "backward"—that is, south. For us it would be like seeing a river flow uphill.

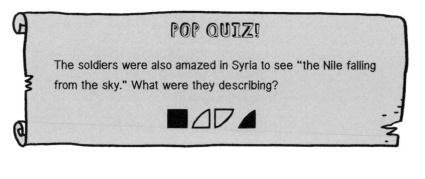

POP QUIZ!

The soldiers were also amazed in Syria to see "the Nile falling from the sky." What were they describing?

COME TOGETHER

Around 3100 BC, Upper Egypt and Lower Egypt were successfully united into one nation. In Egyptian legends the heroic king who did this is called Menes.

The ruler of **Upper Egypt** wore a white crown featuring a vulture (representing the goddess **Nekhbet**).

The ruler of **Lower Egypt** wore a red crown, which featured a cobra (representing their goddess **Wadjet**).

The rulers of a unified Egypt combined the two crowns into one awesome vulture-cobra supercrown—the Sekhmeti, meaning "two powerful ones."

Menes is more of a legendary founder of Egypt than a historical one, like the way the Romans believed that their city was founded by twins named Romulus and Remus.

ARTIST'S IMPRESSION

In reality the king who unified the two Egypts was probably a guy named Narmer, also known as "the Striking Catfish."

After bringing the two Egypts together, Menes or Narmer (or whatever his name was) now ruled over the world's largest unified nation. He was the most powerful man on earth.

EXTRA CREDIT

In one legend about Menes, he was attacked one day by his own dogs while out hunting. Desperate to get away from them, he jumped onto the back of a crocodile, which carried him to safety.

In gratitude to the croc god, Menes went on to found the great city of Crocodilopolis, where you could go to worship sacred, bejeweled crocodiles.

Obviously, the best part of this story is that the ancient Egyptians had a city called Crocodilopolis, which is the coolest thing ever. It's also fun to say. Let's all say "Crocodilopolis" out loud a few times.

GIFTS OF THE NILE

The Greek historian Herodotus called Egypt "the gift of the Nile," because they owed their whole civilization to the river. In fact, "Nile" is a Greek word—the Egyptians just called the Nile *Iteru*, meaning "the river." For them it was the only one in the world!

As Egypt grew into a great nation, the Nile continued to provide the inhabitants with gifts.

In a desert with hardly any trees, you can't build things out of wood. The Egyptians solved that problem by making mud pies! They would bring big lumps of mud and clay in from the Nile wrapped in animal skins. Then they'd add straw and pebbles and pack it into wooden molds. After baking in the sun for almost a month, the mud became bricks that the Egyptians used to build everything, from the lowliest peasant's house to some of the pharaoh's temples.

In the shallow waters by the banks of the Nile, a tall reed called *Cyperus papyrus* ("puh-PIE-russ") grows. As we'll see later on, the Egyptians used the fibers of this plant to make a flat material they could write on. Our word "paper" comes from "papyrus." But the plant was useful in other ways. The poor could eat its roots, or carve them into bowls. It could be burned for fuel. Its hollow stems floated on water so well that Egyptians could bundle them up and make their first boats.

EXTRA CREDIT

In 1969 an adventurer named Thor Heyerdahl built a boat out of papyrus that he used to cross the Atlantic Ocean! He named it the **Ra**, after the Egyptian sun god.

For the most part, the Egyptians thought they lived in the best place in the world and were happy to stay home. But whatever they couldn't get in Egypt, they could trade for along the Nile. From the south the kingdom of Nubia would trade them luxury goods such as elephant ivory, gold, and even giraffe tails to use as flyswatters!

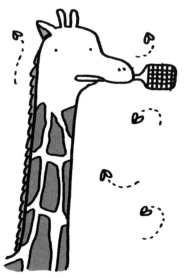

Egypt's trading ships were no tiny papyrus fishing boats—they were made of imported wood, and some were as long as 170 feet, more than twice the size of Columbus's ships. To trade with Asia— bringing cinnamon from

India, for example, or incense from Yemen—merchants had to figure out a way to travel from the Nile to the Red Sea. So they built ships that could be taken apart, carried overland through a *wadi*, or dry riverbed, for 120 miles, and then rebuilt at the coast!

BECAUSE I'M HAPI

The Egyptians even worshipped the Nile River—in the form of the god Hapi. "Fattener of herds!" they would chant. "Might that fashions all! None can live without him!" Hapi was sort of an odd-looking guy. He was bright blue in color, like river water. And to show the life-giving power of the Nile, he was always drawn with women's breasts!

DEEP WATERS

The Nile had its dangers, of course.

For one thing, its path kept moving. Rivers gradually change their courses, and the bed of the Nile River moved east about two or three meters every year. Around 1050 BC, one branch of the Nile made a massive course change, leaving Pi-Rameses, the capital of Egypt, high and dry! The pharaohs built a new capital called Djanet along the new branch of the Nile and ordered the entire temple of Pi-Rameses moved, one stone at a time, to the new site, and rebuilt. Some of the statues that had to be moved weighed more than two hundred tons.

EXTRA CREDIT

"Djanet" is another name for Tanis—the lost Egyptian city that Indiana Jones is searching for in **Raiders of the Lost Ark!**

The ancient Egyptians worshipped crocodiles, but that's mostly because they were so scared of them. And rightly so! To this day Nile crocodiles kill hundreds, maybe thousands, of people in Africa every year. Egyptian sailors had a magical trick they'd try against crocodiles. They'd point at them with their index finger and little finger.

Needless to say, Junior Geniuses, if you're ever facing down a crocodile, I would *not* rely on that trick. It sounds like a good way to get two of your fingers bitten off.

Even more dangerous than the crocodile, believe it or not, is the hippopotamus. If you think hippos are just sleepy, peaceful river lumps, they've got you fooled. Hippos can be aggressive, they're not afraid of people, they run faster than you can, and they like to overturn boats and chomp on people with their twenty-inch-long teeth. Twenty inches? That's about as long as your arm!

In fact, the Egyptians said that their famous first king, Menes, ruled sixty-two years and was finally mauled to death by a hippopotamus. Wow. When you think about it, that's a pretty action-packed way to die for a guy in his eighties.

THE BIRTH OF A NATION

However, the civilization Menes founded lived on *long* after his death. His was just the first of many *dynasties* (royal families) that ruled Egypt over the next three thousand years. Three thousand years! That's longer than Western civilization has lasted, from ancient Greece right up until today.

Let's meet the kings and queens who ran the world for centuries.

SECOND PERIOD

VALLEY OF THE KINGS

Between the reign of Menes and about 30 BC, when Egypt became a Roman province, Egypt was ruled by at least 170 different pharaohs from more than 30 different dynasties. *Don't worry*, Junior Geniuses! I'm not going to make you memorize all those kings and queens and royal families. That would be very boring.

Instead let's squeeze three thousand years of pharaohs into one handy chart. Sorry, your majesties.

Historians group Egypt's many dynasties into longer periods called Kingdoms, when Egypt was stable and powerful. Between the kingdoms were gaps of war and craziness, called Intermediate Periods.

EARLY DYNASTIC PERIOD
(3100-2686 BC)

- EGYPT UNITES
- HIEROGLYPHICS INVENTED
- MENES

THE OLD KINGDOM
(2686-2181 BC)

- PYRAMIDS BUILT

FIRST INTERMEDIATE PERIOD
(2181-2055 BC)

- TOTAL CHAOS

THE MIDDLE KINGDOM
(2055-1650 BC)

- FOREIGN TRADE BEGINS
- AMENEMHAT, SENUSRET

SECOND INTERMEDIATE PERIOD
(1650-1550 BC)

- THE HYKSOS TAKE OVER

THE NEW KINGDOM
(1550-1069 BC)

- THE PEAK OF EGYPT'S POWER AND EMPIRE
- HATSHEPSUT, AMENHOTEP, RAMSES

THIRD INTERMEDIATE PERIOD
(1069-664 BC)

- DECLINE AND DIVISION

FOREIGN RULE (664-30 BC)

- EGYPT CONQUERED BY THE ASSYRIANS, THE PERSIANS, AND THE GREEKS
- ALEXANDER THE GREAT, PTOLEMY, CLEOPATRA

Wow, time sure flies! Feel free to copy this timeline onto a little card and carry it with you at all times, because you never know when Egyptian history will come in handy.

SON OF THE SUN

Egypt's kings and queens referred to themselves with *hieroglyphs* (Egyptian writing symbols) that read "*per-aa*," or "great house." The Greeks pronounced this word "pharaoh," and that's where our word for Egyptian royalty comes from.

JUNIOR GENIUS NITPICK

Actually, the word "pharaoh" just meant "palace" until kings started to use it for themselves early in the New Kingdom. That means that the first one hundred pharaohs of Egypt weren't technically pharaohs at all. I won't tell them if you won't.

The pharaoh was, of course, at the very top of Egyptian society.

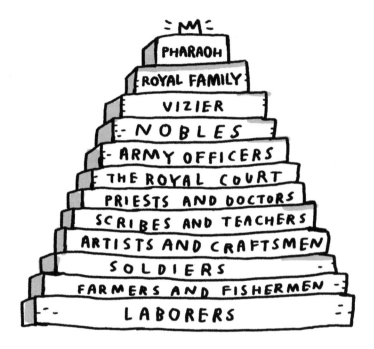

The pharaoh wasn't much like a modern-day world leader, like a president or a prime minister. To the ancient Egyptians, the pharaoh was literally a god. He was the "son of Ra," the earthly manifestation of the sun. He was worshipped with temples and giant statues, and whatever he said was law. When his subjects approached his throne, they kissed the ground—and if they were very lucky, he would sometimes let them kiss his feet as well!

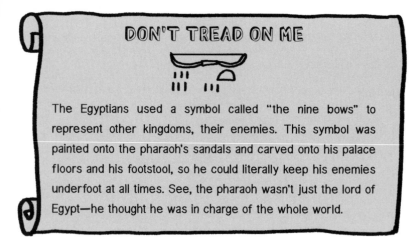

DON'T TREAD ON ME

The Egyptians used a symbol called "the nine bows" to represent other kingdoms, their enemies. This symbol was painted onto the pharaoh's sandals and carved onto his palace floors and his footstool, so he could literally keep his enemies underfoot at all times. See, the pharaoh wasn't just the lord of Egypt—he thought he was in charge of the whole world.

GOOD TO BE KING

The pharaoh lived a life of incredible luxury in his palace. "Gold is as common as dust," wrote a king from the land of Mitanni during the reign of the New Kingdom pharaohs. (Egypt didn't originally have any gold mines, but during the Middle Kingdom it began to trade wheat to Nubia in exchange for gold and other valuables.)

Here are some other perks of being a pharaoh:

SO MANY WIVES! In addition to his queen, the pharaoh kept a harem full of secondary wives and other consorts. Like the pharaoh, his wives had it pretty easy. When a foreign princess named Gilukhipa arrived in Egypt to marry Amenhotep III, she brought along no fewer than 317 servants!

SO MANY KIDS! Rameses the Great had fifty-two sons and even more daughters—which is only possible when you have eight wives and about a hundred concubines.

SO MANY SERVANTS! Each pharaoh had a huge personal staff, from his chief adviser, the "royal vizier," all the way down to little people like the "keeper of the king's nail clippings" and "superintendent of the royal bathroom."

AWESOME PETS! Pharaohs kept tame cheetahs that hunted with them, and trained baboons to pick them fruit. Cats in the royal palace wore golden earrings and necklaces. Talk about Fancy Feast! Rameses the Great even had a pet lion named Anta-m-Nekht ("Slayer of Foes") that bravely fought beside him at the Battle of Kadesh.

EXTRA CREDIT

There's still a breed of dog in Malta today called the "Pharaoh Hound," supposedly descended from the royal hunting dogs of ancient Egypt. Pharaoh hounds are the only dogs that "blush"— when they're happy, they change color and turn pink!

MUSHROOMS! The pharaohs loved the delicious taste of mushrooms so much that they decreed that only royalty was allowed to eat them.

BELLY BUTTON JEWELS! Navel piercing was another sign of power that was off-limits to anyone but the pharaoh.

AIR-CONDITIONING! Special servants were in charge of standing on either side of the pharaoh's throne and fanning him with ostrich feathers.

A PRIVATE BOAT! In 1954 archaeologists discovered a fifty-foot boat belonging to the pharaoh Khufu—which had been disassembled into 1,224 pieces and buried with him! The boat was reassembled like a jigsaw puzzle and now has its own museum.

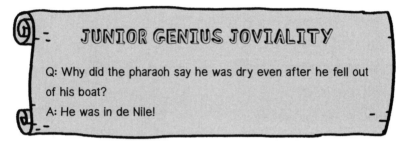

JUNIOR GENIUS JOVIALITY

Q: Why did the pharaoh say he was dry even after he fell out of his boat?

A: He was in de Nile!

A ROYAL PAIN

Life wasn't all mushrooms and belly button rings for the king of Egypt. He also had a lot of work to do. Egypt was divided into forty-two states called *nomes*, and the pharaoh personally owned all the land in all of them. He was in charge of maintaining *ma'at*—an Egyptian word meaning "order" or "balance"—in all his lands. The pharaoh's millions of subjects believed that the sun wouldn't even rise or set if he didn't make it happen.

Controlling the sky is a pretty tough job requirement! But the pharaoh had lots of other responsibilities too. He also had to . . .

KEEP IN SHAPE! Young future pharaohs went through years of athletic training—when you're the son of Ra, you can't be a wimp. The pyramid at Saqqara has the world's oldest sports facility—a private jogging track for the pharaoh. To celebrate his thirtieth year on the throne, the pharaoh would go out to his track and go for a short run

in front of his cheering subjects, to show that he was still fit to be king. He had to keep doing this every three years until he died.

LEARN TO HUNT! Pharaohs such as Thutmose III and Amenhotep III boasted about their legendary hunting ability. We've dug up stone amulets celebrating the 110 lions that Amenhotep personally killed during the first ten years of his reign—as well as the fifty-six bulls he supposedly once bagged in a single day.

LEAD THE TROOPS! During the New Kingdom, pharaohs became war heroes as well. Amenhotep II was said to be such a muscular warrior that his soldiers couldn't even draw his bow. It's said that he once showed off his strength by using three hundred bows in a row to shoot three hundred arrows right through targets of solid copper. And Rameses III's scribes wrote that he once killed 12,535 Libyans in a single battle. (He kept track by cutting off their head or hands as he went.)

KEEP THE PEACE! In 1269 BC, Rameses II signed history's oldest surviving peace treaty, ending a war with the Hittites. A copy of the tablet is now displayed at United Nations headquarters.

ALL IN THE FAMILY

Here's one royal duty that wouldn't go over so well today: lots of pharaohs married their own sisters or daughters! (We're not really sure why—maybe to keep anyone else from fathering a royal rival.) The family trees of the last pharaohs got *especially* complicated. In 80 BC a king named Ptolemy XI Alexander II was forced to marry a woman who was his half sister, his cousin, *and* his stepmother! The marriage didn't last. Alexander murdered his wife/sister/cousin/mom and was promptly killed by his subjects. He reigned for only nineteen days.

ME, A PHARAOH?

Not all pharaohs were born at the palace. Amenemhat I was born a commoner but grew up to found one of Egypt's great dynasties. So hey, maybe you could become a pharaoh someday as well. Here's what you'd look like.

The *nemes*
Egyptian royalty weren't supposed to show their hair, so they wore this striped head cloth.

Kohl
Kings and queens both smeared this black goop, made of crushed lead in animal fat, around their eyes.

A fake beard
The pharaoh was clean-shaven, but he wore this beard to look more like the god Osiris. Cows wore them too!

A *wesekh*
This wide collar of golden beads could be inlaid with precious jewels for bigwigs like the pharaoh.

The *heka* and *nekhakha*
The royal symbol was two scepters—a crook and a flail. Kings were even buried holding them.

QUEENS OF THE NILE

You didn't have to be a man to rule ancient Egypt—but it helped. Only four or five women ever became pharaohs, and it really took some doing.

HATSHEPSUT ran Egypt for more than two decades after the death of her husband, Thutmose II. She wore the whole pharaoh getup—the striped headdress, the false beard. She was even referred to as "His Majesty." Hatshepsut is the first great woman we know about from ancient history.

NEFERTITI was the queen of the pharaoh Akhenaten. Her name means "a beautiful one has come," and a famous sculpture of her head, which you can now see in a Berlin museum, displays her great beauty. Some historians believe that when Akhenaten died, she succeeded him as pharaoh for a few years.

CLEOPATRA is probably the most famous female pharaoh, but she wasn't even Egyptian—she was Greek. In fact, most of the kings in her dynasty, the Ptolemies, didn't speak a word of Egyptian. (Cleopatra did, however. In fact, she spoke nine languages!) To keep her skin looking youthful, Cleopatra bathed in donkey milk every day. It took seven hundred donkeys to keep her bathtub supplied!

POP QUIZ!

According to a famous legend, Cleopatra killed herself in what unusual way?

■◢△◺□◗◹◀□

THEY'RE HISTORY!

Because they were worshipped as gods, the pharaohs also spent a lot of their time erecting statues and temples to themselves. The pharaohs all look strong and handsome in their statues—but we know from their mummies that lots of them were actually balding and overweight. The typical Egyptian diet of beer, bread, and honey made staying in shape back then really hard.

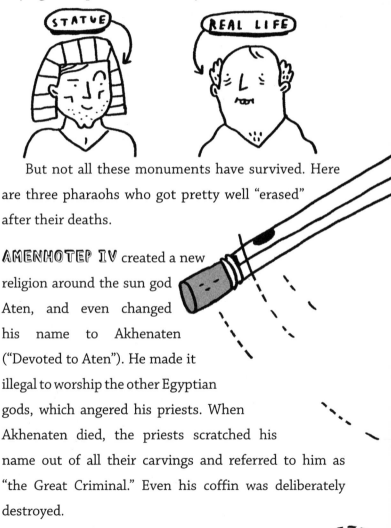

But not all these monuments have survived. Here are three pharaohs who got pretty well "erased" after their deaths.

AMENHOTEP IV created a new religion around the sun god Aten, and even changed his name to Akhenaten ("Devoted to Aten"). He made it illegal to worship the other Egyptian gods, which angered his priests. When Akhenaten died, the priests scratched his name out of all their carvings and referred to him as "the Great Criminal." Even his coffin was deliberately destroyed.

AMASIS II had it even rougher! When Cambyses II of Persia conquered Egypt and became pharaoh, he ordered that the body of his predecessor, Amasis II, be brought to him. Then he beat it, stabbed it, and plucked out all its hairs! The corpse was already embalmed, so Cambyses wasn't able to do much damage. Finally he ordered it burned.

QUEEN HATSHEPSUT wasn't loved by her stepson, Thutmose III. He took the throne by claiming that a statue of the sun god Amun had come to life in the temple and proclaimed him king. Then he built a big wall around Hatshepsut's monuments so no one could even see them, hoping that she'd be forgotten! Ironically, this wall preserved them beautifully for thousands of years.

GAME OF THRONES

Who was the oldest pharaoh? The youngest? The smartest? The meanest? It's time to hold a competition among all 170 pharaohs of Egypt and find out. I've brought ribbons to give out as prizes.

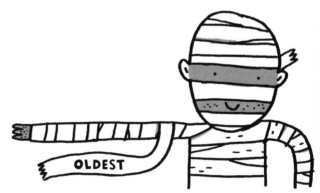

OLDEST

Pepi II ruled Egypt for ninety-four years. The average life span in Pepi's day was so short that his feat would be like living to be two hundred today! He sure put the "Old" in "Old Kingdom."

YOUNGEST

Tutankhamen, aka King Tut, is called the "boy king" of Egypt because he took the throne when he was only nine! He died when he was about eighteen, but we're not sure how. (The Egyptologists who discovered Tut's tomb cut the corpse up to get it out of his coffin! So it's a little late for an autopsy.) In 2006 scientists made some new scans of King Tut's body and determined that he probably broke his leg in a chariot accident, and then died when the wound got infected.

FASTEST

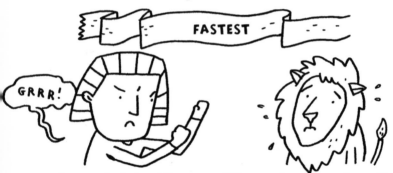

GRRR!

It's recorded that Thutmose III once slew seven lions "in the blink of an eye." Heck, I would have been impressed by just one.

LAZIEST

Taharqa once made his soldiers go for a thirty-mile run in the desert—while he rode alongside in his chariot.

CRUELEST

Khufu may have built the world's biggest pyramids, but he was not a popular guy. Some histories say that he closed the Egyptians' temples and "brought them to every kind of suffering."

VAINEST

More than half the ancient Egyptian monuments that currently survive were built by a single king, Rameses the Great. His reign was so long that he outlived twelve of his own sons, and his thirteenth son, Merneptah, was already an old man when he succeeded his father.

BRAINIEST

Hatshepsut has been called history's first zoologist and botanist. She sent servants south to the land of Punt and ordered them to bring back different types of trees, as well as animals such as rhinos, giraffes, and leopards.

SLEEPIEST

The Hyksos, "shepherd kings" from Asia, ended the Middle Kingdom when they took over Egypt around 1650 BC. The Egyptians hated the Hyksos, but the invaders did bring new inventions with them, such as chariots and bronze. The Hyksos king Apepi demanded that the people of Thebes get rid of their hippopotamus pool, because all the hippo noise was keeping him up nights. The Theban king refused, and the war that resulted eventually kicked the Hyksos out of Egypt.

Actually, Junior Geniuses, the pharaohs were super-rich and powerful and probably don't care about little ribbons or prizes. But they did enjoy playing games. Let's play some ancient Egyptian games now, at recess! I'll see you back here at your desks in fifteen minutes.

RECESS

In 1160 BC, the Egyptians held the first international sports event in recorded history. In this Iron Age Olympics, Egypt's soldiers took on foreigners at sports such as wrestling and quarterstaff duels. But those sports seem a little violent to me, Junior Geniuses. I won't allow any wrestling or stick fighting at recess.

We know from tomb paintings that young Egyptian boys played a more innocent game—tug-of-war! Unfortunately, they didn't use a rope—they linked hands and tried to pull one another's arms apart. Okay, let's not play that one either.

Here are some fun three-thousand-year-old games that are hopefully safe enough so that no one winds up in a sarcophagus.

KHUZZA LAWIZZA

Khuzza lawizza! What a wonderful phrase. *Khuzza lawizza*—ain't no passing craze! This game is an old Egyptian version of leapfrog. Two players sit on the floor facing each other, extend their arms out in front, and touch hands. A third player tries to jump over their outstretched arms. Yell "*Khuzza lawizza!*" if the leap is successful, because that is fun to say. Keep raising the bar and take turns seeing who can jump the highest!

JUMP THIS WAY

THE EYE OF APOPHIS

Almost 4,500 years before Babe Ruth, the Egyptian pharaohs played a kind of baseball called *seker-hemat*—as a religious ritual! In a temple courtyard they'd use a stick to whack at a ball that represented the eye of Apophis, an evil serpent from their myths. Whacking the "eye" was a way to defeat the serpent and keep *ma'at* (order) in the land.

Have one player be a "pharaoh" with a bat and a Wiffle ball. (He or she can toss the ball in the air and swing at it, or use some kind of tee. There's no pitcher.)

The other players are "priests" in the field. The pharaoh gets one point for every time he can hit a ball toward the priests without someone catching it. (The ball has to travel in the air as far as the nearest priest, or it's not a point.) Switch pharaohs after every successful catch.

SENET

One of the world's oldest board games, Senet (the "Game of Passing") was so popular in ancient Egypt that there are paintings of Queen Nefertiti herself playing it. Tutankhamen was even buried with four Senet boards.

The rules of Senet (as far as we can guess) were a little bit complicated, but I bet you'll soon get the hang of it. You and a friend can use the board on the next page, or a copy of it.

LET'S PLAY
SENET

OKAY!

Each player gets five tokens. You could use ten chess pawns (five white and five black) or spare change (five dimes and five pennies). At the start of the game, players alternate their tokens along the first ten squares, or "houses."

Instead of dice the Egyptians used "throwing sticks." Take four Popsicle sticks and color one side of each, so each stick has a light side and a dark side. Players take turns tossing the sticks into the air. On your turn move any one of your tokens one space for each stick that landed light side up. (For four dark sides, move five spaces, not zero.) Your own tokens cannot be in the same square. If the number of moves would have you land on an opponent's token, the tokens swap places. (If you can't find a legal move, just skip your turn.)

There are five houses marked with special symbols:

House of Happiness. All tokens must land directly on this square before they can move on. If your throw is so high that your token would go past square 26, you must choose a different piece to move.

House of Water. If you land on this square, you drown and must move your token back to the **House of Rebirth** (square 15, with the ankh symbol). Tokens that get sent backward by an opponent advancing from the House of Happiness drown in the House of Water.

House of the Three Truths. A token that lands here is trapped until you throw a three. Then it leaves the board.

House of Ra-Atum. A token that lands here is trapped until you throw a two. Then it leaves the board.

The first player to clear all of his or her tokens off the board wins!

THIRD PERIOD

PYRAMID SCHEMES

The Egyptian pharaohs built lots of great monuments to themselves, but they *all* looked pretty lame compared to the biggest ego trip of them all—the amazing pyramids of Giza!

These giant triangular tombstones were built by the pharaohs of Egypt's fourth dynasty. The greatest of all of them was the pyramid of a king named Khufu (also known as "Cheops" to the Greeks). This pyramid was built more than 4,500 years ago, so long ago that mammoths were still living off the coast of Siberia. But even today it would be an engineering marvel.

The Great Pyramid of Khufu . . .

◦ **Weighs more than six million tons.**

◦ **Covers 13.6 acres of ground—about seven modern city blocks.**

◦ **Contains enough masonry to build a road from New York City to San Francisco.**

◦ **Was the tallest building on earth for almost 3,800 years!**

481 FT — THE GREAT PYRAMID

316 FT — BIG BEN

305 FT — the STATUE OF LIBERTY

THE LEANING TOWER OF PISA — 184 FT

HOMEWORK

Which buildings where you live are shorter than the Great Pyramid? Are there any that are taller?

In 2012 a French architect estimated that, even using modern technology, it would take five years and more than five *billion* dollars to build the Great Pyramid today! (Luckily, we already have one, so we can save our money and not do this.)

So how did the kings of Egypt—a nation that hadn't even invented the wheel—manage to build such massive monuments? And why? To find out, Junior Geniuses, we have to travel even further back in time—to the creation of the world.

NU ORDER

The ancient Egyptians believed that the universe was a vast, dark, watery abyss called Nu. Our world was born when a mound called the Benben rose from the waters

of Nu. This was where the first creator god sat. His name was Atum, and he created Shu (the god of air) and Tefnut (the goddess of water) by spitting them out of his mouth. Yuck.

Atum was a sun god, and the pharaohs of the Old Kingdom believed that he lifted their souls up into the stars when they died. So the giant tombs they built were pyramid-shaped to symbolize the mound of Atum, and they were so tall because they represented the pharaohs' stairway to heaven. In fact, the Egyptian word for pyramid was "*mer*," meaning "place of ascension."

THE SAHARA DESSERT

Our word "pyramid" comes from the Greek "**pyramis**," which probably originally referred to a kind of wheat cake with a pointy top. That's right. The ancient Greeks saw pyramids and said, "Hey, those things look kind of like our cakes!" This is why I refer to trees as "giant broccoli" and to the sun as "that big yellow Corn Pop in the sky."

NAME THAT TOMB

Almost 120 royal pyramids have been discovered by archaeologists, but many are just ruins by now. Recently, seventeen new ones were discovered using infrared imaging from satellites, which can see things that have been buried by sand.

EXTRA CREDIT

The country of Sudan actually has more pyramids than Egypt! These pyramids, from the ancient land of Nubia, are much smaller than their Egyptian cousins.

By studying these sites, we've discovered that it took the Egyptians a while to figure out how to make pyramids as cool as Khufu's.

BEFORE THE OLD KINGDOM, each Egyptian king was buried in a sloped building called a *per-djet,* or "house of eternity." Today we call them *mastabas*, an Arabic word meaning "stone benches."

BURIAL SHAFT

MASTABA

DJOSER, a king during the third dynasty, wanted something a little fancier, so he stacked six mastabas on top of each other, making the first *step pyramid*.

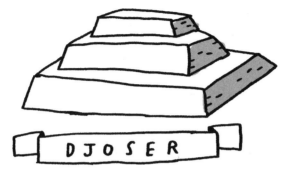

SNEFERU, the founder of the next dynasty, built this unique *bent pyramid*. This was probably an attempt at a smooth-sided pyramid that had to be changed midway through construction because the original angle was too steep—the pyramid would have collapsed.

Sneferu's next attempt was the nearby "Red Pyramid." This time the construction was more stable and the first *true pyramid* was completed. Sneferu's son Khufu went on to build the biggest true pyramid in history.

THE FIRST JUNIOR GENIUS

The very first pyramid, the tomb of Djoser, was probably the brainchild of a guy named Imhotep, the first scientist known to history. In the *Mummy* movies Imhotep is an evil high priest, but the real Imhotep was smart and multitalented. One inscription lists eight different job titles for Imhotep, so he must have had a pretty big business card.

IMHOTEP

- CHANCELLOR OF THE KING OF LOWER EGYPT
- FIRST AFTER THE KING OF LOWER EGYPT
- ADMINISTRATOR OF THE GREAT PALACE
- HEREDITARY LORD
- GREATEST OF SEERS
- BUILDER
- SCULPTOR

Imhotep was also history's first doctor, diagnosing and treating more than two hundred different illnesses, from tuberculosis to gallstones to arthritis. A thousand years later his name was still remembered in Egypt, and three thousand years later the Greeks and Romans worshipped him as a god!

HOW TO BUILD A PYRAMID

Building a giant pyramid is fairly straightforward, Junior Geniuses. I'm surprised some of you haven't already tried it at home. Here are eight easy steps to remember.

1. SHIP the rock to your building site six hundred miles away using river rafts. Wheeled vehicles have not been invented yet, so on land you'll need to tow the stones on giant sleds, wetting down the sand as you go to make it slippery.

2. LEVEL thirteen acres of land so it's perfectly flat. Use the floodwaters of a nearby river—it makes the surveying much easier!

3. HIRE thirty thousand workers. (It's often said that slaves built the pyramids, but Junior Geniuses should know better! Archaeologists have found graffiti near the pyramids made by crews bragging about their work. It seems they were skilled laborers who needed work during the non-flood months of the year, when there was nothing to do in the fields.) Here's a hot tip from a pharaoh named Senusret II: Try moving your whole capital city to your pyramid site, so everyone can pitch in!

4. ARRANGE stones into a perfectly square foundation. Remember to align your square precisely with true north, like Khufu did! His pyramid is correct to within one twentieth of a degree, which is more accurate than the observatories of London or Paris.

5. LIFT the other two million stones hundreds of feet into the air without cranes or pulleys. (Remember, the biggest ones weigh about fifteen tons—as much as two

elephants!) Helpful hint: Build a quarter mile of wooden ramps forty stories high!

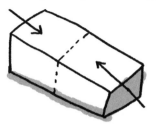

6. PLACE the blocks together so tightly that not even a human fingernail can fit between them.

7. CONTINUE to add a new block every few minutes for *the next twenty years.*

8. TA-DA! You've got yourself a pyramid!

PHEW!

People have been inventing theories about the pyramids for thousands of years, and most of them were baloney! Here are some of my favorite crackpot ideas about the pyramids. Remember, there are grown-ups walking around who actually believe this stuff.

They were built using kites! In 2001 a Caltech aeronautics professor used giant kites to lift a four-ton tower, called an obelisk, into place. Could this be how the pyramids were built?!

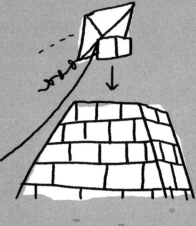

They are giant faucets! Some ~~weirdos~~ people think that the pyramids were hydraulic pumps. Could the burial chambers and passageways inside the pyramids actually be ancient water pipes?!

They are giant yardsticks! In 1859 a publisher named John Taylor hated the metric system. He wrote a book claiming to prove that the pyramids had been built by Noah (yes, the ark guy) using good old-fashioned British inches! Could this be Noah's way of warning us against the metric system?!

They are power plants! Other pyramid nuts think that the pyramids somehow converted the earth's energy into electricity. Could the ancient Egyptians have used this power to levitate in midair, just like the lost people of Atlantis?!

They were built by aliens! This one is true. Aliens built the pyramids. Finally, it feels good to come clean. Now, if you'll excuse me, I must return to my home planet.

I NEVER GET CREDIT FOR ANYTHING.

INSIDE INFORMATION

I understand why people make up nutty theories about the pyramids. They're so big and mysterious! What's inside them? Are they solid? Hollow? Filled with a delicious creamy center?

Let's go inside and find out.

PYRAMID OF KHUFU

The king's chamber
Where Khufu's sarcophagus rested in peace

The queen's chamber
We know now this name is misleading, because the queen was actually buried in another pyramid nearby. This room may have held a statue of the king's soul.

The lower chamber
Why was this spooky dead end carved into the bedrock below the pyramid? It's a mystery.

Relieving chambers
These five compartments helped distribute the pyramid's weight, so the ceiling wouldn't collapse on poor Khufu.

Narrow shafts
Were these for air, or did they serve a religious purpose, like letting the king's soul rise to heaven?

The grand gallery
The vaulted roof here is an architectural masterpiece.

The ascending passage
This passage was hidden behind a limestone wall, in hopes of outsmarting grave robbers.

The entrance
Sealed up tight once the pharaoh was placed inside

EXTRA CREDIT

Today scientists investigating the mysteries of Khufu's tomb have a new tool—pyramid-crawling robots! Miniature robots exploring the vertical shafts in the "queen's chamber" have found a series of secret doors with copper handles and painted red hieroglyphics. What do you think is up there?

ROCK CITY

Have you ever heard the expression "as silent as the grave"? Well, the pyramids may have been giant six-million-ton graves, but they weren't silent at all. They were hopping! Remember, Egyptians considered their kings to be gods, so commoners would continue to worship at the tombs of dead pharaohs. Whole cities would grow up to support the dead king's priests and servants.

The *necropolis* ("city of the dead") at Giza wasn't just the three big pyramids. There were also thousands of other tombs, from massive ones for the royal family to simpler graves for workers who had helped build the pyramids. Each pyramid had a temple or two on the east side—always on the east side, so the pharaoh could be reborn like the rising sun.

At the entrance to the Giza necropolis sits the famous Great Sphinx, the largest *monolithic* (carved from one rock) statue in the world. The statue was already thousands of years old before the Greeks decided to call it a "sphinx." It was probably designed to represent the pharaoh Khafra, who's buried in the second-largest pyramid nearby.

The Sphinx was buried in the desert sand for centuries—and it might still be there, if not for a king named Thutmose IV. Thutmose was out hunting one day as a boy and stopped to take a snooze in the shadow of the Sphinx. In a dream he was told that he would become pharaoh if he dug up the statue and restored it—so he did. Unfortunately, modern pollution is slowly dissolving the Sphinx. It might have been better off staying under the sand!

The Sphinx in Greek myth was famous for asking riddles, but I have a riddle I'd like to ask the Sphinx.

There are marks on the Sphinx's face where the nose was pried away with chisels. (There's an old story about Napoleon Bonaparte's army blowing it off with a cannon, but that's just a myth.) One Arab historian says that a local holy man chipped it away in 1378, because he thought the local peasants shouldn't be worshipping a statue. Officials promptly hanged the holy man for vandalism.

Is this story true? Nobody nose.

POP QUIZ!

Napoleon was fascinated by the pyramids and calculated that the Great Pyramid of Khufu contained so much stone that it could be used to build a ten-foot-high wall all the way around his whole country! (Luckily, he never actually tried this out.)
What country did Napoleon rule?

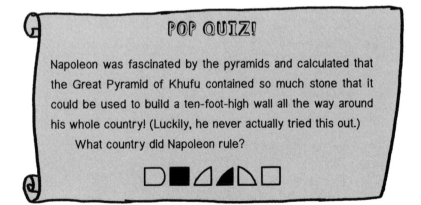

THE WONDER YEARS

The ancient Greeks kept a list of the most amazing things ever built in the classic world. Today we call these places the Seven Wonders of the Ancient World.

	Location	Destroyed By
Lighthouse of Alexandria	Alexandria, Egypt	Earthquake
Colossus of Rhodes	Rhodes, Greece	Earthquake
Mausoleum at Halicarnassus	Bodrum, Turkey	Earthquake
Statue of Zeus at Olympia	Olympia, Greece	Fire
Temple of Artemis at Ephesus	Izmir, Turkey	Fire and plunder
Hanging Gardens of Babylon	Hillah, Iraq	Earthquake
Great Pyramid of Giza	Giza, Egypt	Nothing!

As you can see, it's not possible to visit most of the Seven Wonders anymore. The Temple of Artemis, for example, was burned down *twice*—once by a guy named Herostratus, who hoped the act would make him famous. Instead the Ephesians executed him and made it a capital crime ever to speak his name out loud!

(Oops. I just said "Herostratus." Twice! Don't tell the Ephesians.)

But one of the wonders still survives: the pyramid of Khufu at Giza. It outlasted the other six by almost one thousand years, and it's still going strong.

In 2001 a Swiss foundation called New7Wonders announced its plan to select a new list: seven wonders of the *modern* world. More than one hundred million phone votes were cast, making it the biggest poll in history. When Egypt complained that its wonder shouldn't have to compete against a bunch of newcomers like the Great Wall of China, the Colosseum in Rome, and the Taj Mahal, the Great Pyramid was granted an honorary eighth spot on the list.

HIGH LIGHT REEL

You might have noticed that the Egyptians had a second building on the Seven Wonders list—the Lighthouse of Alexandria, or the Pharos. When it was built by the Ptolemies, the last pharaohs of Egypt, around 250 BC, it was the second-tallest structure in the world (after Khufu's pyramid, of course). It lasted until the fourteenth century, when it was ruined by a series of earthquakes.

The Pharos looked more like a skyscraper than a modern lighthouse. The giant lamp on top of it (a reflective mirror during the day and a fire by night) could be seen from twenty miles away. Above the lamp was a statue of Poseidon, the Greek god of the sea.

The lighthouse was designed by a Greek architect named Sostratus, but Ptolemy II, the pharaoh, wouldn't let Sostratus take credit for his work. So Sostratus cleverly carved his name into the stone of the lighthouse, then covered it over with plaster that said "Ptolemy II." In time the pharaoh's name wore away and only Sostratus's name remained! Let's hear it for Sostratus, the master of very, very slow revenge.

BACK IN THE DAY

The pyramids of Giza aren't the Pretty Good Pyramids. They are called "Great Pyramids" for a reason. They are man-made mountains, each thirty times as massive as the Empire State Building. But check it out. These wonders of the world were even *more* wonderful four thousand years ago! Here's why.

1. THEY WERE TALLER. Khufu's pyramid was 481 feet tall when it was built. Today it's only about 450 feet, thanks to erosion and visitors stealing stones from the *pyramidion*, the pyramid's peak cap.

2. THEY WERE FULL OF TREASURE. Despite all the dead ends and secret passageways, every single pyramid had been looted of all its gold by 1000 BC. Many of these thefts were probably "inside jobs" done by priests stealing the very treasures they'd sworn to protect.

3. THEY GLOWED LIKE CRAZY. All three of the Giza pyramids were originally covered in polished white limestone, which must have been blindingly bright

under the hot desert sun! Today this smooth outer casing is gone, mostly "borrowed" in the last thousand years to build homes and mosques in nearby Cairo.

The pyramids have been looted, worn down, and stripped away, but they're still magnificent. Even today, if the Great Pyramid of Khufu had its little pyramidion back, it would be taller than any building in north Africa.

In thousands of years we'll all be gone, but the pyramids will still be there. As the Arabs say, "Man fears time, but time fears the pyramids."

ART CLASS

The reeds of the papyrus plant were so plentiful in the Nile delta that the hieroglyph meaning "papyrus" was also the symbol for "Lower Egypt." It looked like this:

But an actual papyrus plant looks more like this.

Papyrus can grow about ten feet tall, and the Egyptians made dozens of products from its triangular stalks: rope, floor mats, baskets, sandals, furniture, and more. But the most important thing they made was paper.

Papyrus changed the world, because it was the best stuff to write on for almost five thousand years, until the Chinese invented hemp-fiber paper around 100 AD. The pharaohs kept the method of making papyrus a closely guarded secret, so Egypt could trade it to other lands. Lots of documents from all over the ancient world, including much of the Bible, were originally written on papyrus.

We're going to make our own version of papyrus today. First go look out the window. I bet you don't see any papyrus reeds nearby, right? No problem. We'll substitute some other ingredients. You'll need:

PAPER CUT INTO ONE-INCH STRIPS

TRAY OR PAN

WATER

FLOUR

WHISK

WAXED PAPER

ROLLING PIN

1. First, put a cup of flour and two cups of water into a tray or shallow pan. Stir well with the whisk until the mixture is smooth.

2. Now you need to dip your strips of paper into the flour-water mixture until they're well soaked. You can use regular typing paper, or strips from a paper bag if you want darker papyrus. Egyptian papyrus was made with strips of *pith*—the yellow tissue at the center of papyrus stems—so construction paper in a color like yellow or tan will probably be the most realistic.

3. One strip at a time, lay the goopy paper strips side by side on the waxed paper. (They can even overlap a little.) The Egyptians wouldn't have needed flour, of course. Their paper was held together by the sticky sap of the papyrus plant as it dried.

4. Now that you have a row of vertical strips, add another layer on top, horizontally. This will give you the crisscross pattern we see in Egyptian papyrus.

5. Cover your "papyrus" with another sheet of waxed paper and roll the rolling pin firmly and evenly over the top to squeeze out the water and flatten your papyrus. (The Egyptians would have used stone hammers.)

6. Carefully peel off the top sheet of waxed paper and leave your papyrus out to dry.

FOR EXPERTS ONLY

When you're done, you can glue multiple sheets of papyrus together in a line and then roll them up to make a scroll. The longest Egyptian papyrus ever found is in the British Museum, and it's 134 feet long!

7. Once your papyrus is dry, grab some paint or markers to decorate it. One thing you might draw is a *cartouche*. A cartouche is like a name tag worn by a pharaoh. It would

 contain the hieroglyphs for his or her royal name, set inside an oval, like this.

An amulet with the pharaoh's cartouche would be placed in his tomb, so his soul wouldn't get lost and would be protected from evil spirits.

Would you like to write your name in hieroglyphs? That's a little complicated. There were more than five thousand hieroglyphs, and the Egyptians wrote down only consonants, not vowels. We say that the Egyptian word for beautiful is "*nefer*," like in Nefertiti, but that's just a guess at how to pronounce it. The hieroglyphics just say "nfr." Think how much time that would save on a spelling test!

But if you had to pick one symbol that was closest to each English letter, they might look something like this:

Try signing your own name. My cartouche ("KEN") would be:

Or like this—because hieroglyphs were often written right to left!

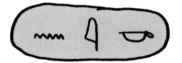

Now my soul won't get lost! This is very important. I'm always losing things.

FOURTH PERIOD

RITE OF THE LIVING DEAD

In ancient Egypt life was hard and short. Most people didn't live to see their fortieth birthday. So people thought a lot about the afterlife—that's when the party would really begin! No poverty, no sandstorms, no scorpion bites. And if you were royalty, of course, you'd be hanging out with the gods.

That's why the Egyptians prepared so carefully for the next world and created such elaborate tombs and death rituals. This is very lucky for us, Junior Geniuses. Thanks to these records and relics, we actually know more about how ancient Egyptians died than how they lived!

TAKE FIVE

All of the Egyptian death practices arose from one belief:
Everyone has a soul, but it comes apart into five pieces,
like a model kit or a LEGO set.

THE KA
Your life force, your
breath. Fueled by eating
and drinking.

THE NAME
Your identity, which
must be protected. The
oval around a cartouche
is a rope protecting your
name from harm.

THE BA
Your personality—
whatever makes
you, you.

THE AKH
After death the
ka and *ba* reunite
to form the *akh*,
a kind of ghost
on its way to the
afterlife.

THE SHADOW
In life your shadow
is stuck to your feet,
but after death it has
a life of its own.

The Egyptians believed that these five parts of the soul left the body when it died. They would only come together again if the body was taken *very* good care of. And that's how we finally get to:

Come on. I know you bought this book for the mummies.

FINALLY, MUMMIES!

You young people are all full of life and health, but let's face some gross facts for a minute: Someday, when we die, our bodies won't stay in good shape for very long. We're full of bacteria, and once we're not breathing anymore, the bacteria take over. Within four to six days dead bodies start to turn weird colors (green, then purple, then black) and start leaking and puffing up and smelling funny. If there are bugs nearby, a corpse can get stripped down to its skeleton in fewer than two weeks!

Yuck. The only bodies that miss out on all that fun are ones that have been *mummified*. That means that something happened to preserve the body. Sometimes nature makes mummies. The peat bogs of Europe are so cool and acidic that bacteria can't thrive there, so perfectly preserved humans, called "bog bodies," are often found down in the mud. Lots of hot, dry desert sand can do the same thing.

That's probably how the ancient Egyptians first discovered mummification. Our word "mummy" comes from the Persian word *"mumiya,"* meaning "asphalt." Asphalt, like the black stuff that roads are paved with. The Egyptians used asphalt-like resins to fill up the empty spaces inside a mummy after its organs were removed.

That's right; they removed the organs! I hope you have a strong stomach, Junior Geniuses, because we're about to find out how the Egyptians made people into mummies. It takes *way* more than a roll of masking tape.

EXTRA CREDIT

One of the greatest fears of an ancient Egyptian was dying outside of Egypt. They believed that if their body didn't get mummified, it would miss out on the afterlife.

GETTING PRETTY IN TENTS

Around 3400 BC the Egyptians figured out that leaving a body in a sand pit isn't the best way to make a mummy. You can also preserve it with chemicals. This process is called *embalming*.

The Egyptian embalmers worked in special tents way out in the desert. This had two advantages:

1. It kept their mummy-making methods secret.

2. It kept the bad smells away!

Let's take a tour.

IBU
The Place of Purification

Bodies were first brought here to be washed in water and palm wine. *(Fifteen days.)*

WABET
The Palace of Embalming

The organs were removed and the body dried out by packing it with salt. *(Forty days.)*

PER NEFER
The House of Beauty

The mummy was wrapped in as many as twenty layers of linen. Archaeologists have found one mummy with three miles of bandages! *(Fifteen days.)*

MUMMY MANAGEMENT

The embalmers would act out religious rituals and perform spells while they worked on the body. The chief embalmer acted as Anubis, the jackal-headed Egyptian god of the dead.

ANUBIS

But these were not just priests—they were skilled medical workers as well. The Egyptians' great surgical and anatomical knowledge probably began with the art of making mummies.

In the Palace of Embalming a priest called the "ripper-up" would make a careful incision in the side of the body. This was a necessary step, but it was seen as very disrespectful to the dead, so the other priests would make a show of angrily chasing the "ripper-up" away, as if he'd done something wrong!

The heart was believed to be the center of thought and feeling, so the dead got to keep that for the afterlife. But all the other organs were removed from the body cavity. They were placed in special containers called *canopic jars* that represented the four sons of the god Horus.

LUNGS	STOMACH	LIVER	INTESTINES
HAPI	DUAMUTEF	IMSETI	QEBEHSENUEF
(BABOON)	(JACKAL)	(HUMAN)	(FALCON)

The Egyptians mistakenly believed that the brain's only purpose was making *mucus* (snot!) for the nose, so they didn't treat it very well during mummification. Prepare to be grossed out: They stuck a metal hook up the corpse's nose, stirred the brain into liquid, then drained it out through the nostrils!

POP QUIZ!

There wasn't really any top secret recipe for preserving the body. The mummy was just stuffed with a salt called **natron**, mostly made up of soda ash and sodium bicarbonate—which you probably have in your kitchen right now! What is sodium bicarbonate?

□△▽△◁ ■◻■□△

Apart from getting a giant hook shoved up their nose, the dead were treated very well, because the goal was for the embalmed person to look just like he or she had in life. It was almost like a spa day!

Moisturizers! Oils, wax, and spices were rubbed into the skin as it dried out.

Nose job! Rameses II had his nose stuffed with peppercorns to keep its distinctive shape.

Eye treatments! Sometimes a mummy's eyes were replaced with onions. I bet there was lots of crying at the funeral.

AHHH... THIS IS tHE DEATH...

Hair care! Mummies got their hair done as they dried out! Some even got false hair made of string so they'd look their best in the tomb.

Botox! Linen, mud, or sawdust could be pushed under the mummy's skin to plump it up a bit.

EXTRA CREDIT

Despite all that work, mummies' faces did end up pretty discolored and shriveled up. The monster played by Boris Karloff in the old movie *The Mummy* was based on the actual face of Rameses III's mummy. It took Karloff eight hours a day to get into his mummy makeup!

WRAP SESSION

Once the deceased was all dried up and ready to go, the House of Beauty took care of the final step, wrapping the body in cloth. Rich people got covered in brand-new linen, which was an expensive commodity back then. But mummification was available to everyone in ancient

Egypt, not just the pharaoh. Regular Egyptians got wrapped up in scraps of linen ripped up from old clothes! How come horror movies never show a lower-middle-class mummy, dressed in hand-me-downs and Grandma's pillowcases?

The body was covered so carefully that each finger and toe received its own individual wrapping. To this day, many of these mummies still have their fingernails and toenails perfectly preserved by their five-thousand-year-old manicures!

The beauticians in the House of Beauty were also in charge of slipping magical amulets in with the bandages to protect the dead on its way to the afterlife. On the chest they'd usually place a special *scarab*—a stone carved like a beetle.

The scarab was supposed to cover the heart. That way the heart couldn't reveal its guilty secrets to the god Osiris when the person was judged.

Often the embalmers would place a copy of *The Book of the Dead* between the mummy's legs. The Egyptians believed that as the soul passed through Duat, or the underworld, it would have to pass through many perils, such as:

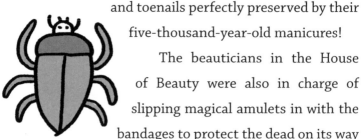

a lake of fire　　**poisonous snakes**　　**executioners**

The Book of the Dead was like a treasure map or a book of cheat codes for Duat. It contained spells that would lead the soul safely to the next world.

EXTRA CREDIT

There are 189 different spells in various versions of **The Book of the Dead**. The very last one is a spell designed to protect the dead Egyptian from eating animal poop! I think we can all agree that is a very useful spell to have, Junior Geniuses.

SAY "AH!"

The last step of mummification was one of the most important—the ceremony called the Opening of the Mouth. The Egyptians believed that the dead person's *ka* would need food and drink in the next world, but how was a wrapped-up mummy supposed to eat? So the last thing the embalmers did was to put a slit in the mummy's bandages with a special snake-shaped knife. This was the moment that supposedly brought him or her "back to life."

THINKING INSIDE THE BOX

Most Egyptians would just be wrapped in mats or placed in simple clay coffins before they were buried in the sand. But if you were rich or royalty, you got something a lot more elaborate, a stone coffin called a sarcophagus.

Early pharaohs were placed in sarcophagi shaped like houses or palaces—so they'd feel right at home, I guess. Later sarcophagi were carved to look like the mummy inside. This way the dead soul could always find its way back to the right body.

The Eye of Horus, so the mummy could see what was going on.

Protective spells

Maps and underworld gods painted on the inside, so the dead wouldn't get lost.

MAN CAVE

Pharaohs had the sweetest coffin setups of all. When Tutankhamen's tomb was discovered, he was lying inside a solid-gold coffin, nested inside two more coffins of gilded wood, nested inside a stone sarcophagus, nested inside four large golden shrines! The outermost shrine was nine feet high and sixteen feet long, big enough to hold a car. The innermost coffin was 296 pounds of 22-karat gold. Melted down, it would be worth about $2 million! But let's not do that. In its current form, it's priceless.

GRAVE DANGER

After the person's mummified body was placed in the sarcophagus, the coffin was then carried to its final resting place in a big procession. The family would show their grief by weeping loudly and tearing their clothes. If they couldn't make enough noise, professional mourners were hired to join in the sadness. Women waved their arms in the air and threw dust over their hair. At the door of the tomb, performers called *muu* put on reed crowns and did a silent dance.

It took so long to dig a tomb that one of the first things a pharaoh did when he took the throne was pick out the place where he wanted to be buried. During the New Kingdom period, royal mummies were buried in the Valley of the Kings, a small canyon surrounded by steep cliffs across the Nile River from the ancient capital of Thebes. More than 130 different tombs have been found in the area, many of which are very elaborate. The tomb of Queen Nefertari has been called "the Sistine Chapel of Egypt" because of the beautiful paintings on the walls and ceiling.

JUNIOR GENIUS JOVIALITY

Q: Why did the mummy have a hard time falling asleep in his tomb?
A: Because he'd gotten all wound up!

All these tombs were secret, carved deep into the rock and hidden away for centuries, in hopes that they'd be safe from thieves. Robbing tombs was a boom industry in ancient Egypt. In theory the Valley of the Kings was protected by the cobra goddess Meretseger, who would poison invaders. The penalty for grave robbing was harsh: death by impalement! But in practice, officials mostly looked the other way while millions of dollars of gold and gems disappeared into the desert. Sometimes the tomb guards themselves were responsible.

Even the famous tomb of King Tut didn't go untouched. Archaeologists think that at least 60 percent of its contents were looted thousands of years ago. They've even found the fingerprints of robbers on oil vessels in the tombs! Talk about a cold case.

EXTRA CREDIT

Not all these thieves were master criminals. Scientists have unwrapped some mummies that turned out to have a second head or a third leg under their bandages. This was a result of robbers unwrapping a bunch of mummies to steal stuff, getting their parts all mixed up, then rewrapping them in a hurry to make a quick getaway!

YOU CAN'T TAKE IT WITH YOU

The reason why Egyptians were buried in big tombs is the same reason why people sometimes buy big houses—to hold all their stuff!

It's a long journey to the next world, the ancient Egyptians figured. So you have to be prepared. Here are some of the supplies the pharaohs packed into their tombs.

HONEY

TOILET

SELF-PORTRAIT

CAT MUMMY

DOG MUMMY

SOUL HOUSE

CLOTHES

Self-portraits. Kings would put statues of themselves in their tombs, so their *ka* and *ba* would have someplace to hang out if the body got a little moldy.

Snacks. We know honey never spoils, because we've found pots of it in ancient Egyptian tombs, and it's as good as new. Even Twinkies don't have that kind of shelf life!

Clothes. Well, you wouldn't want to be naked when Osiris judged you, would you?

Robot helpers. If you didn't want to work in the next life, you would bring along little figurines called *shabti* to do the dirty work. Some people would be buried with 365 different *shabti*, one for every day of the year.

Non-robot helpers. Sadly, some servants were killed by early Egyptian kings and then buried with them! I guess it's nice to know you'll have job security . . . forever.

Transportation. Some kings brought along giant funeral barges, painted green to symbolize new life. King Tut was buried with six chariots—which is a little weird, since he may have died from a chariot accident.

"Soul houses." These were little model homes where your *ka* could live. If it was really, really tiny.

Toilets. No comment.

A private zoo. The kings of Egypt often had mummified animals buried with them. Sometimes these were companions—household pets, baboons, snakes, mice, fish, and even a crocodile with its babies placed in its jaws. But sometimes the animals were preserved . . . as jerky. Tutankhamen, for example, had forty boxes of meat buried with him. One scientist says it still looks pretty yummy four thousand years later: "The poultry looks like you've just gone to Safeway and bought a roast bird!"

RAIDERS OF THE LOST BARK

We're not sure why, but the Egyptians were big on mummifying animals. In Saqqara there was a whole tomb for bulls, and in 1888 three hundred thousand mummified cats were pulled out of a cemetery in Bubastis, the city of the cat goddess. Just a few years ago a secret catacomb of tunnels was discovered that contained the mummies of eight **million** dogs!

WHERE ARE THEY NOW?

The Egyptians had a very specific idea of what would happen to them after they died. Anubis would weigh

their heart against the feather of Ma'at, the goddess of truth.

If the heart was pure, the soul could ascend toward Osiris. But if the heart failed

on the scale, the soul would be swallowed by Ammit, the

"Devourer of the Dead."
Ammit was a terrible
monster who combined
the three most deadly
Egyptian beasts—the
lion, the hippo, and the
crocodile.

Even a giant brain like mine doesn't know what happened to the Egyptians' souls, Junior Geniuses. That's beyond the scope of science. But we can trace what's been happening lately with their dried-out bodies. The mummified cats found in Bubastis met a sad end. They were shipped to England and used as fertilizer. Here are some of the other fun adventures that a pharaoh might enjoy after his or her death!

Become great art! Lots of nineteenth-century artists used a paint color called Mummy Brown—made of ground-up mummies! When the English painter Edward Burne-Jones discovered that his tube of brown paint was made from mummies, he promptly buried it in his garden.

Wrap packages! During a Civil War linen shortage, a paper mill in Maine bought a whole bunch of mummy wrappings to make into paper. It didn't work, so they just sold the mummy linen as gift wrap.

Cheat the sick! In the 1600s, European doctors claimed that eating powdered mummies (yum!) could cure everything from bruises to stomachaches.

Power a train! When the British were building railroads in Egypt, it was said they burned mummies to fuel their steam locomotives.

Be a party game! It was fashionable in Victorian England to buy a mummy for your dinner party and let your guests take turns unwrapping it.

Wave to the nice people! When Rameses II's mummy was unwrapped, his left arm sprang upward, scaring the bejeebers out of a roomful of scientists.

Pay taxes as a fish! In 1881 a batch of mummies was shipped to Cairo to be displayed in a museum. City officials were unsure how to fill out papers for the cargo but finally decided to tax them in the closest category available—"dried fish."

Become a crime scene! In 2011 rumors spread in Egypt that the throats of mummies contain a magical substance called "red mercury." Several museums have been broken into by looters looking for the mysterious stuff.

Watch the Super Bowl! Tulane University stored two mummies under its stadium bleachers, which means they were there for three of the first nine Super Bowls.

See Europe! In 1974 the mummy of Rameses the Great had begun to deteriorate a bit, so Egypt sent it to France to be studied. Rameses traveled first-class, though! He was even issued an Egyptian passport, which gave his occupation as "King (deceased)."

And with that, Junior Geniuses, I think we can consider our lesson on mummies . . . all wrapped up. It's time for lunch!

LUNCH

From the lowliest peasant to the pharaoh himself, the ancient Egyptians were crazy about bread. Wheat was the "staff of life" that fueled their civilization, and during the Middle Kingdom they even used bread as a unit of measure and currency, instead of money. Rather than getting five bucks for a job, a worker might be paid five loaves' worth of stuff. Egypt loved carbs so much that the Greeks called them "the bread eaters."

The Greek writer Herodotus scoffed that the weirdo Egyptians "kneaded bread with their feet," but it's a good thing for us that they did. Some historians think that's how leavened bread was first invented! The Egyptians might have discovered that bread turned out lighter and fluffier when they kneaded it with their feet—because the baker might

have had a yeast infection between his toes, and yeast makes bread rise! Yuck.

There was one downside to eating so much bread. Sand gets everywhere in the desert, and Egyptian bread often had a lot of grit in it left over from the process of making flour. A lifetime of eating sandy bread would scrape up and  wear away people's teeth—even the pharaohs' teeth! We know from studying his mummy that Amenhotep III was a dentist's nightmare. He may have been the sun god incarnate, but he probably didn't smile very much.

Here's a lunch idea that combines two Egyptian favorites—baked goods and corpses.

YUMMY MUMMIES

INGREDIENTS

1 TUBE REFRIGERATED BREAD DOUGH

1 PACKAGE HOT DOGS

3 SLICES AMERICAN CHEESE

COOKING SPRAY

KETCHUP AND MUSTARD

Directions

1. Preheat your oven to the temperature specified on the tube of dough (probably 350° or 375°). This recipe uses an oven and a sharp knife, so get help from a grown-up, or you might face the wrath of the pharaoh.

2. Lay the dough flat. Then use a kitchen knife or pizza cutter to slice it into a series of narrow strips, half an inch wide or less.

3. Cut each slice of cheese into four strips. Place each hot dog on a strip of cheese.

4. Wrap several dough strips as "bandages" around each hot dog and cheese strip. Leave a gap about half an inch from the end of the hot dog—this will be the mummy's face.

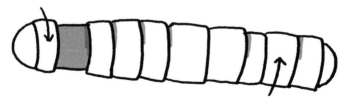

5. Place your mummies on a cookie sheet about half an inch apart. Embalm them lightly with the cooking spray.

6. *Seal the pyramid!!!* (Close the oven.) Keep an eye on your mummies to make sure they don't come back to life and make trouble. Within 12–16 minutes (depending on the kind of dough you used) they should be turning a light golden brown, and then it's time to raid the tomb.

7. After your grown-up helper removes the mummy tray from the oven, use a toothpick to put two dots of mustard on your mummies' faces for eyes. Once they're cool, serve the mummies with little "canopic jars" of ketchup and mustard for dipping.

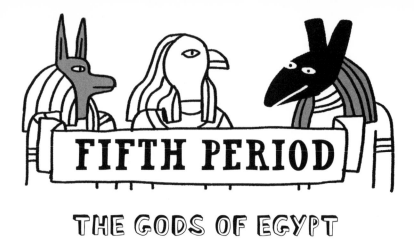

FIFTH PERIOD

THE GODS OF EGYPT

As you might recall from the Junior Genius Guide to Greek mythology, the ancient Greeks had well over a dozen gods, and it was all pretty confusing. I had to make some charts. Well, the Greeks were slackers compared to the ancient Egyptians, who worshipped more than *two thousand* different gods and goddesses.

I'm not going to make a chart of them. It would be too long.

Why so many? Well, our version of Greek mythology is a pretty consistent story hammered out over the centuries. The Greeks were like TV or comic book geeks. They spent a lot of time trying to fit all their stories together and explain how they were consistent.

But the stories we have about the Egyptian gods are

fragments pieced together much later from scrolls and temple paintings. They're myths from many different regions, some hundreds of miles apart, and from many different time periods, some thousands of years apart.

NOME MERCY

Each of the forty-two nomes (districts) of Egypt had its own god, which is part of the problem. There were also forty-two different demons—one for each nome—who judged the dead in the Hall of Two Truths. (Everyone got quizzed about their lives, like on a game show, before Anubis weighed their hearts.) That was nice. No matter where you were from, you'd always see a demon from your hometown.

That's why sometimes the sun god in Egyptian stories is Ra, and sometimes it's a guy called Amun or Atum or Khepri or Horus. Sometimes it's even a hyphenated combination.

RA   AMUN   ATUM   HORUS

AMUN-RA   ATUM-RA   RA-HORAKHTY

Sometimes the cow goddess Hathor is described as Ra's mother. Other times she's his sister or his daughter.

You just have to learn to live with the contradictions, Junior Geniuses.

EXTRA CREDIT

The chemical ammonia, which gives lots of cleaning products their sharp smell, was actually named by the Romans because they first mined it near an Egyptian temple to Amun. They called it **sal ammoniacus**—"the salt of Amun."

BRINGING THE HEAT

When you live in a blazing-hot place like Egypt, I guess it makes sense that your chief god would be the sun. What's more powerful than the desert sun?

The sun brings light, warmth, and growth, so the sun god Ra was a creator. In one myth he cries tears of joy that fall to earth. Where the tears hit the soil, the first men and women were created.

But just as the sun can brutally scorch the land, Ra was also a destroyer. The "Eye of Ra" was a weapon that could be used against humanity. In one story, Ra gets fed up with the evil stuff that people are doing, so he sends out his Eye to destroy them. The Eye spends the day wreaking havoc, but all the violence makes Ra change his mind. To end the massacre Ra dyes some beer red and pours gallons of it all over the land. The Eye drinks the red beer, believing it's blood, and winds up too sleepy to hurt any more people. The human race is saved by food coloring!

EXTRA CREDIT

Ra isn't the only creator god. In some myths Ra's rival is Ptah, often drawn as a mummy. Ptah creates the world and everything on it just by having an idea—everything he thinks of magically appears. In other stories, the first people are sculpted out of clay by the ram-headed god Khnum, using a potter's wheel.

The many Egyptian sun gods were usually identified with Ra at different times of day.

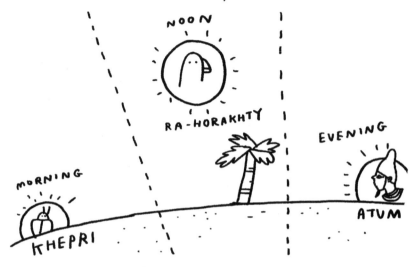

The sacred Egyptian scarab beetle was actually an insect that we know better as the dung beetle. As you might guess from their name, dung beetles are really into poop. They roll poop into a massive ball that they roll around everywhere, until they either eat it or lay their eggs in it. Gross.

For the Egyptians the sun rolling up out of the horizon at dawn reminded them of the scarab rolling its poop, so Ra's aspect at sunrise was Khepri, the beetle god. At noon the sun was Ra-Horakhty, watching over the land from high overhead like a falcon. In the evening it was Atum, the oldest of all the gods.

The Egyptians pictured Ra sailing overhead in his vessel, the Boat of Millions of Years. But at the horizon he switched to his evening boat and traveled all night across Duat, the underworld, battling monsters. This is why the Egyptians buried their dead in the western part of the country. The sun set there, so they associated it with the underworld.

Ra never got a break. He spent all night battling the giant serpent Apophis, who had great coils, a head of flint, and a magical hypnotic stare. Every night Ra was victorious, and the sun was reborn in the east.

HOMEWORK

Ra's scepter was a shape called the **ankh**, which symbolized eternal life to the Egyptians. It could be combined with the pillar-shaped symbol **djed**, which represented stability, or the staff-shaped **was**, meaning power.

ANKH

DJED

WAS

Egyptians would often carry little amulets around with them, hoping that the charms would ward off evil and bad luck. To protect him from drowning, a ferryman might carry an amulet in the shape of a fish. A funny-looking ape-man named Bes—the only Egyptian god drawn face-on—might guard your sleep against nightmares. A **djed** amulet on your back would protect it from injury. Everyone wore these little charms, from babies to corpses.

Use whatever materials you want—cardboard, foil, paper, clay—to make an amulet of your own, using Egyptian symbols. Ward off the modern-day evil of your choice— dodgeball, old computer, bedhead. Just think of all the terrible things that could happen if you don't have a pocket full of amulets!

CREATURE FEATURE

Even if the sun was in charge, the Egyptians were like the Greeks: They had a whole *pantheon* (collection) of gods and goddesses.

LIKE THE GREEK GODS, THEY WERE ...	UNLIKE THE GREEK GODS, THEY WERE ...
Powerful and immortal	Mostly friendly and benign
All related, like a big family	Not into blood sacrifices
Worshipped at home and in temples	Depicted with animal heads

That's right, animal heads.

ANUBIS
DOG
God of the Dead

BASTET
CAT
Goddess of
Music and Dance

HATHOR
COW
Goddess of
Love and Motherhood

HORUS
FALCON
God of the Sky

KHEPRI
SCARAB
God of the Sunrise

SEKHMET
VULTURE
Goddess of
Fire and War

NEKHBET
LION
**Goddess of
Upper Egypt**

SET
???
God of Storms

SOBEK
CROCODILE
God of Water

TAWERET
HIPPO
**Goddess of
Childbirth**

THOTH
IBIS
God of Scribes

WADJET
COBRA
**Goddess of
Lower Egypt**

Did the Egyptians think that if they ever ran into Sobek, he would actually have a big crocodile head on his shoulders? Or did they just draw and sculpt him that way to represent his fearsome power as a river god? The truth may be somewhere in between. The Egyptians thought of their gods as very mysterious.

Other gods were always drawn as human, including most of the family of Atum.

THE TOP TEN

Atum was the creator god in the Egyptian city of Heliopolis. We've already learned how he spat the air god Shu and the moisture goddess Tefnut into being. Shu and Tefnut went on to have their own children: the earth god Geb and the goddess Nut, who represented the canopy of the sky stretching overhead. Shu eventually separated the two (which is why today there's air between the earth and the sky) but not before they'd had children of their own: Osiris, Isis, Set, and Nephthys.

These nine gods are called the *ennead* of Egyptian mythology. That's actually a Greek word meaning "a group of nine." You know how the Three Musketeers were a trio and the Beatles were a quartet? Well, the Greek word for nine of something is an *ennead*. Now you know.

GREEK TO ME

Much of what we know about Egyptian myth comes from what the Greeks recorded when they first traveled to Egypt. So some of the Egyptian gods are known today by names that are really the Greek versions. For example, the Egyptians would have no idea who "Isis" is; they called her "Aset." "Osiris" was really named "Usir."

Sometimes a tenth member was included in the ennead—*Horus*. Here's his story.

FAMILY REUNION

Osiris ruled Egypt in peace and order alongside his queen, Isis. But their brother, Set, became jealous and wanted to take the throne. So Set devised a trick: He built a wooden chest and announced that he would give it as a gift to whoever fit perfectly inside it. When

Osiris lay down in the chest to try it out, Set sealed it shut and drowned his brother in the Nile. Then, just to make sure Osiris stayed dead, Set divided his body into pieces, scattering them all over Egypt. There were forty-two parts, one for every province. Set was a very thorough guy.

Isis and her sister Nephthys flew over the land like falcons, searching for Osiris and weeping. (That's why the annual flooding of the Nile was always referred to as "the tears of Isis.") Finally they collected

all forty-two parts of Osiris's body and put him back together, returning him to life. This legend was acted out for thousands of years in Egyptian mummification rituals, with the dead king representing Osiris.

Osiris, after his journey through death, became god of the underworld—but not before giving his queen, Isis, a son.

EXTRA CREDIT

Osiris is usually depicted wearing a crown of reeds and ostrich feathers. His weirdest feature is his skin, which is colored a very dark green. This represents the fertile soil of the Nile valley, where he ruled.

HE WHO IS FAR ABOVE

With Osiris gone to rule over the underworld, Isis hid from Set in a thicket of papyrus near the Nile until she gave birth to her son. She named him Horus, meaning "falcon" or "he who is far above." Set sent snakes and scorpions to kill the boy, but Isis protected him.

When Horus grew up, he was pretty steamed at Set about the whole ripping-apart-his-dad thing, and challenged him for the throne. It was an epic confrontation.

ROUND 1. A river battle, in which both gods turned into hippos.

ROUND 2. A fight in which Set stole Horus's left eye.

ROUND 3. A court case before the entire *ennead*, which Horus won by planting evidence on Set's favorite food—a head of lettuce!

ROUND 4. A boat race, which Horus won by tricking Set into making his boat out of stone. (Set doesn't seem to be the smartest of the gods.)

ROUND 5. A massive battle between Horus's armies and Set's forces.

This lasted eighty years, but finally Horus defeated his evil uncle and reclaimed the throne. In one version of the story, the god Thoth magically restored Horus's missing eye, which Horus then offered to Osiris. The Eye of Horus, or *wedjat*, became one of the most powerful magical symbols of the ancient Egyptians.

SET: A GOOD EXAMPLE

After his defeat, Set got a new job. He became the bodyguard of Ra! He stands on the helm of the solar boat with a spear, keeping away Apophis, the serpent of chaos.

HOLY COW!

Because they associated their gods with different creatures, lots of animal life was sacred to the Egyptians. Here's a countdown of the . . .

Top Five Egyptian Animals NOT to Mess With

5. BEES. Because beeswax and honey were such important products, bees were called the "tears of Ra."

4. HIPPOS. The hippo goddess Taweret was the goddess of childbirth. Pregnant women would wear amulets of a mean-looking female hippo to keep trouble away.

3. BULLS. The cult of Apis worshipped the sacred bull of Ptah, a bull that had a black forehead with a white triangle, a scarab mark under its tongue, and twenty-seven other specific marks. If a calf had every single mark, he would be chosen to live a life of luxury, with his very own temple and a whole "harem" of female cows.

2. DUNG BEETLES. Remember? With the poop? We already covered this.

1. CATS. The Egyptians loved their pet cats so much that when one died, the whole household would go into mourning, and everyone would shave their eyebrows. The penalty for killing a cat—even accidentally—was death.

TEMPLE RUN

In ancient Egypt, if you needed advice from one of the gods, you could just pay them a visit. That was what temples were for! If you were sick, you could take a nap in the temple of Hathor and hope that the goddess would send you a healing dream. If you were in need, you could leave a carved stone ear in Ptah's temple, and maybe he'd hear your plea.

See, the Egyptians believed that the gods literally lived in the stone temples the pharaohs built, in the form

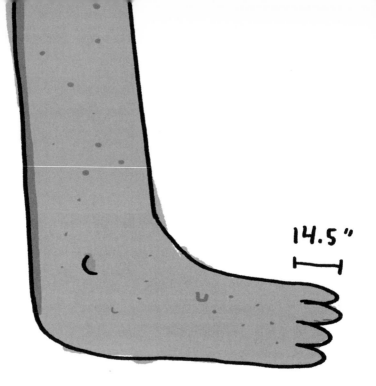

14.5"

of statues. These statues were *enormous*. In the ruins of one temple at Djanet, a big toe was found that measured more than a foot across.

The statue probably would have been sixty-five feet tall, visible from miles away. Today these statues are just faded limestone and granite, but in ancient Egypt they were painted in dazzling colors.

If a statue was smaller, the priests would treat it as if it *were* the god himself. Let's see how your daily ritual compares with an Egyptian god's.

YOU	STATUE
Woken up by an alarm clock, or an annoyed grown-up saying, "You're late for school!"	Woken up by a priest repeating the words "I am a pure one!" as he broke the clay seal and entered the god's shrine
Quick bath or shower	Sprinkled with water from a sacred lake
Maybe some hair product or body spray?	Dabbed with perfume, while incense was burned to make his shrine smell better
Pull a shirt and jeans on.	Draped by the priests in brightly colored linens. Then came the makeup and the jewels!
Quick bowl of cereal	Bread, fruit, vegetables, and meat were spread before the statue. (The priests and their families ate very well on the "leftovers.")
Glass of orange juice	Temple floors had trenches so worshippers could pour out some beer or wine for the statue.

During the day the priests would leave personal items such as mirrors scattered around the temple in case the god needed them. The statue got three big meals a day before getting tucked into bed for the night.

The pharaoh was a god too, so technically he was supposed to be in his own temple 24/7. But he had other important royal duties, so he'd usually have a painting or a statue to substitute for him.

SPECIAL EFFECTS

The temple of Abu Simbel was designed so that sunlight would beam into the sanctuary on only two days of the year, to celebrate the birthday and coronation date of Rameses II. It would illuminate the statues of all the gods—except Ptah, who stayed in the dark because of his connection with the underworld.

The statues in Amenhotep III's temple had an even better trick: At dawn they were rumored to give off a strange noise, like whistling or a lyre string breaking. Could this have been the sound of water evaporating inside the quartzite rock? Or just a hoax put on by the priests? It's a mystery to this day.

RA POWER

Egyptian temples were designed to get across the mystery and awe of the gods, so they were *big*. Big and dark. And the temple to Amun-Ra at Karnak, outside Thebes, was the very biggest.

Not a lot of temples to Amun survive, because new pharaohs would often tear down old temples and use the materials to build new ones, hoping Amun would be flattered at having a new place to live. But five thousand years later, Karnak is still around—too big to recycle!—and gets almost a million visitors every year.

KARNAK

EASTERN TEMPLE

TEMPLE OF PTAH

OPEN COURT

SACRED LAKE

AVENUE OF SPHINXES
1,350 ram-headed sandstone sphinxes lining the road to the temple of Luxor, a mile away

TEMPLE OF KHONSU

TEMPLE OF RAMSES III

GREAT HYPOSTYLE HALL
So big it could hold Paris's Notre Dame cathedral. Rows of reed-shaped pillars so big that fifty people could stand atop each one.

SHRINES AND CHAPELS
Amun's golden statue was hidden away in a dark sanctuary here—but once a year, during the Opet festival, it was carried to Luxor in a sacred boat.

At its peak the Karnak complex controlled:

81,000 WORKERS

422,000 CATTLE

590,000 ACRES OF FARMLAND

433 GARDENS

85 SHIPS

65 VILLAGES

Temple priests (or *hem netjer*—"servants of god") had a pretty cushy job. To stay ritually clean there were some tough requirements. They had to bathe four times a day and pluck out *all* their hair—even their eyelashes!

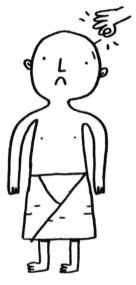

But in return they could tell the country what the will of the gods was (and in the meantime enjoy an all-you-can-eat buffet of the gods' food). That's a lot of power.

Eventually Karnak's high priests of Amun got *too* big for their britches. (Bonus fact: They did not wear britches. They wore long skirts.) The priests controlled more than half of the land in Egypt, and had more power than the pharaoh himself! This eventually led to the collapse of the New Kingdom.

For centuries Thebes was the capital of Egypt. Then the Assyrians invaded Egypt and sacked the whole city. Today ruins of the temples at Luxor and Karnak are all that remain of what was once the largest city in the world.

MUSIC CLASS

The ancient Egyptians loved music. We've found paintings of flutes and harps being played at parties, of workers tapping rhythm sticks and other percussion instruments as they stomped grapes, of acrobatic dancing at public celebrations. We even have a record of a song farmers used to sing to their cattle:

You have driven the oxen on all the roads.
You have walked over the sand.
Now you are trampling on the grass.
You are eating the rich plants.
Now you are satisfied. May it become your bodies well.

Catchy! That song would obviously be a huge radio hit, even today.

The household god Bes was the god of music, but goddesses such as Hathor and Isis were often pictured holding a special instrument called the sistrum. A sistrum was like a rattle, but it was used in religious rituals to keep away evil. Worried about evil spirits? Cobra in the house? Nile flooding? No problem! Shake your sistrum!

If you have a lot of worries, maybe you should build a sistrum of your own. Make a handle out of a Y-shaped branch and string a couple of wires across the two ends. (I recommend twisting floral wire or jewelry wire around the wood, and then covering any pointy ends with duct tape.) Put any kind of noisemakers you want on the wires: beads, bells, or washers, for example. Take old bottle caps and punch a hole in them with a screwdriver. Anything you want.

You now have an Egyptian sistrum! You're ready for anything. Rain at your softball game? Shake your sistrum at it! Kid on the school bus making fun of your hat? Shake your sistrum at him! Violent stomach cramps and vomiting? Okay, that one you should probably see a doctor about because it might be food poisoning.

Sadly, we have no idea what the ancient Egyptians' music sounded like, because they didn't write it down. All we can do is look at pictures and guess. That's hard. It's like trying to figure out what a band sounds like when all you have is the album cover.

THIS NIRVANA BAND MUST SOUND LIKE A SWIMMING BABY.

In 1922 a pair of trumpets—one silver and one bronze—was found in the tomb of Tutankhamen, and plans were made to sound them for the first time in three thousand years. But when a British army trumpeter tried to play the silver one for King Farouk of Egypt, it shattered! The trumpet was restored to be played over BBC radio, but right before the broadcast the power went out in Cairo. The curator at the Cairo museum still claims that the trumpets have "magical powers."

SIXTH PERIOD

LIFE ON THE NILE

Our images of ancient Egypt mostly come from the rich and powerful. A kid like Tutankhamen, for example, wore jeweled sandals and had golden statues made of himself, all before he was even old enough to shave.

But of course most Egyptians didn't live like that! If you wanted to find out how the average family lives today, would you study magazine articles about movie stars and Internet billionaires? Egypt had many desperately poor people as well as rich ones. King Tut's famous death mask came from the mines of Wawat, where slaves would have had to crush eleven thousand tons of rock to yield that much gold.

Most people in ancient Egypt weren't pharaohs or slaves. They were commoners with regular jobs: farmers, soldiers, fishermen. They had normal clothes and houses, and shoes without jewels on them. Let's find out what your life would have been like if you'd been born along the Nile River a few thousand years ago.

LITTLE HOUSE ON THE DESERT

About a hundred years ago archaeologists began to excavate Deir el-Medina, a village that the Egyptians called Set Maat (the "place of truth"). This village is where laborers lived for hundreds of years while digging the tombs in the nearby Valley of the Kings. We've learned a lot about daily life in ancient Egypt by studying the homes of Deir el-Medina.

If you grew up in an ancient Egyptian village, your house would be made of mud bricks painted white on the outside, to reflect the blistering heat of the sun. It was probably about three hundred or four hundred square feet in size. Today the average new American house is twenty-three hundred square feet. A whole

Egyptian home would fit in a modern living room! And I hope you like your neighbors, because houses were very close together in Egyptian towns. Streets were often so narrow that you could reach all the way across just by spreading out your arms.

Inside, your floor was probably dirt, with straw mats for carpets or for sitting on. There was probably no kitchen (the roof was flat, so you could cook up there) or bathroom (you, um, took care of that outside too). Not much furniture either . . . maybe just a few baskets for storage. You probably slept on the floor—or on the roof when it got too hot inside—on a straw mattress with a nice stone headrest for a pillow. Comfy!

If you did have a bed, it was probably as uncomfortable as your pillows were. For some reason the Egyptians

liked beds that sloped downward, so your feet were a little lower than your head. These beds needed footrests, or else you might slide right off.

EGYPTIAN MAKEOVER: HOME EDITION

Wealthier Egyptians' homes had luxuries such as tile floors, stone walls, wood and leather furniture, and servants' quarters. Often the house would surround a central courtyard with a pool in it, full of fish and flowers. If you were very rich, you might even have a toilet! (Well, a wooden bench with a hole in it, over a bowl of sand.) Fancy!

LOOKING HOT

So you wake up on the roof after a refreshing sleep on a stone pillow. Time to get ready for the day! Here's the rundown:

Get dressed. If you're little, this will take about zero seconds. In ancient Egypt young kids just ran around naked! If you're a little older, it's a wraparound skirt

for boys and a floor-length dress with shoulder straps for girls. During the New Kingdom, simple tunics (like long T-shirts) became popular. Before then, shirts basically hadn't been invented yet.

Check your hair. This will be quick too. Egyptian kids kept their heads shaved, except for one braided sidelock. Grown-ups, even women, also went bald. Hey,  it was cooler and prevented lice. Wigs were made of human hair and were held on with beeswax.

EXTRA CREDIT

The hieroglyphic symbol for "child" was actually just a picture of the S-shaped "sidelock of youth."

Fix your makeup. Everybody wore kohl on their eyes, even babies. Kohl was kept in little pots shaped like monkeys. It was supposed to reduce the sun's glare, and probably prevented eye infections too.

A little perfume. It's going to be hot out there, Junior Geniuses. Luckily, Egypt has invented deodorant! Well, sort of. It's a cone made of scented grease that you put on your head! As the sun melts the grease, it drips fragrance down your body all day.

Sandals! Before you leave the house, don't forget your shoes! To take them off, that is. Egyptians usually wore sandals at home but went around barefoot outside.

SHOUT STAINS OUT!

One of the most dangerous jobs in ancient Egypt: laundryman! People washed their clothes in the Nile, which was full of crocodiles, hippos, and parasites. So you were literally taking your life in your hands every time you put in a load of whites. If your mom gives you a hard time about laundry, count your blessings, Junior Geniuses. At least there are no crocodiles in your washing machine.

MEET THE PARENTS

Egyptian kids played with toys not too different from yours. We've found clay and leather balls, toy boats, marbles, dolls, and little tops that they'd spin with papyrus twine. But it wasn't all fun and games back then! Today we wouldn't think much of ancient Egyptian parenting. It was common for moms and dads to . . .

Call kids by animal names! Do you remind mom of a frog or a monkey? Well, great. Everyone is going to call you Frog or Monkey from now on.

Pack beer in kids' lunches. Beer—actually a thick goopy stuff made from fermented bread dough—was a common drink for kids.

Find kids a full-time job. In Egypt only about one person in a hundred knew how to read. So unless you were in training to be a scribe, which started at age four, you just skipped school and started working—in the fields, or in Dad's pottery shop, or whatever. It was even tougher on girls, who often got married around age twelve.

CAN'T HOLD US DOWN

Women in ancient Egypt actually did okay, compared to societies in Greece or Rome. They were allowed to:

- **Own property**
- **Divorce and remarry**
- **Make wills and contracts**
- **Serve on juries and testify in court**

Some women worked outside the home for the same pay as men. When they got married, they were allowed to sign a "prenup"—an agreement to protect their property. And a husband who mistreated his wife was in big trouble. He could get one hundred lashes with a whip.

WORK LIKE AN EGYPTIAN

So you're six years old, you live in ancient Egypt, and you need a job. The work schedule back then was a long one. Their week was ten days long, so people would work nine days in a row, followed by one day off. Workers would put in four hours every morning, then come home during the heat of the afternoon, then go back to work in the evening. If you decided not to go home for a nap, you could pack a sack lunch. The most common quick midday meal: a loaf of bread, some beer, and an onion.

Workers in Egypt weren't slaves (except for the *actual* slaves, who were mostly prisoners of war) and could demand better wages from their bosses. In fact, the first strike in recorded human history took place in 1150 BC, when laborers building tombs for Rameses III staged a sit-down strike to get a raise.

But there were no coins in Egypt until the Persians invaded around 500 BC, so a laborer's paycheck would come in the form of grain, oil, or linen. The real measure of wealth was cattle. The pharaoh would hold a cattle-

counting census every two years to see how much tax everyone owed.

Please allow me to be your ancient Egyptian guidance counselor so we can find you a career.

DO YOU LIKE . . .	YOU SHOULD BE A . . .
Going around naked?	Manual laborer! It was so hot that most of the guys building tombs and temples for pharaohs wore only their birthday suits.
Trained monkeys?	Police officer! Egyptian cops trained dogs and monkeys to help them fight crime.
Hitting business rivals with poles?	Fisherman! "Water jousting" was common, with fishing boats trying to knock rival crews into the Nile.
High heels?	Butcher! Egyptian butchers got to wear heels at work, to keep their feet clean as they cut meat.
Crocodile poop?	Doctor! According to medical knowledge back then, smearing a patient in crocodile poop was a great way to cast out demons.

WEIRD SCIENCE

If you plan on moving to ancient Egypt, I highly recommend not getting sick. Egyptian medical knowledge was a weird mix of science and superstition. Doctors knew that willow leaves would reduce pain (that's how aspirin was discovered) and moldy bread placed on a wound could prevent infection (that's penicillin). We've even found a papyrus from 3000 BC with suggestions on how to treat cancer! Surgery was performed with pieces of volcanic glass almost as sharp as today's scalpels.

On the other hand, if you had a cold, Egyptian doctors might prescribe you breast milk from a woman who had just given birth to a son. For a cough, you'd have to eat a live mouse. If you had arthritis, they might even have zapped you with an electric catfish!

EXTRA CREDIT

Just like physicians today, ancient Egyptian doctors had specialties. There were eye doctors, stomach doctors, even dentists. The pharaoh had his very own proctologist—Iri, the "keeper of the royal rectum."

ROCK, SCISSORS, PAPYRUS

Without Egyptian doctors, we wouldn't have s'mores today! They were the first to discover that marshmallow plants had a sweet, sticky sap, which they used as cough medicine. (Probably because they didn't have graham crackers or chocolate.)

Marshmallows aren't the only thing we can thank the ancient Egyptians for. Here's my list of . . .

Top Ten Most Surprising Egyptian Inventions

Scissors. The first Egyptian scissors were two blades connected by a thin strip of bronze that would bounce back when the blades were squeezed.

Lettuce. A dandelion-like herb was cultivated into the leafy green we eat in salads today. The Egyptians loved lettuce so much that they even worshipped a god of lettuce, called Min!

Hockey. Long L-shaped palm stalks were used to roll a small ball around. This crude form of field hockey is still called *hoksha* in Egypt today.

The color blue. Well, obviously there were already blue things around. Like the sky and, um, bluebirds. But Egypt invented the world's first synthetic pigment, "Egyptian blue," which they used in paints and to color ceramics.

Toothpaste. The world's first toothpaste was made of ox hooves, burned eggshells, volcanic rock, and an oil called myrrh. Minty fresh!

Tic-tac-toe. The Egyptians were already playing three-in-a-row games around 1300 BC.

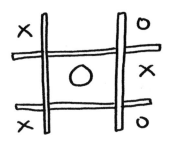

Artificial limbs. In 2000, Cairo scientists discovered the oldest prosthetic body part ever found—a wooden toe placed on a mummified woman three thousand years ago.

The hour. Egypt is the first place where the twenty-four-hour day was ever used. But they never figured out leap year, so their calendar got about a month out of whack every century. "Winter is come in summer, and the months come about turned backward!" one farmer complained.

Cinderella. The oldest known version of the Cinderella story was told by the Greeks about an Egyptian princess, Rhodopis. An eagle drops her shoe into the lap of the king, who then scours the kingdom for the girl who fits the shoe.

Fig Newtons. The Egyptians trained monkeys to pick figs for them. Sometimes they'd make a paste of the figs and bake it in pastry. Presto! The first fig roll.

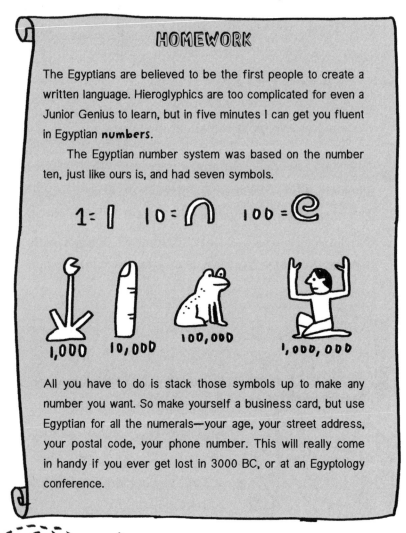

HOMEWORK

The Egyptians are believed to be the first people to create a written language. Hieroglyphics are too complicated for even a Junior Genius to learn, but in five minutes I can get you fluent in Egyptian **numbers**.

The Egyptian number system was based on the number ten, just like ours is, and had seven symbols.

1 = │   10 = ∩   100 = ⊚

1,000   10,000   100,000   1,000,000

All you have to do is stack those symbols up to make any number you want. So make yourself a business card, but use Egyptian for all the numerals—your age, your street address, your postal code, your phone number. This will really come in handy if you ever get lost in 3000 BC, or at an Egyptology conference.

SEVENTH PERIOD

THE SANDS OF TIME

For centuries the Egyptians were the most advanced civilization on earth, but they kept mostly to themselves. And why not? They thought the Nile valley was the greatest place in the world. They didn't need to bother their neighbors.

That all changed during the New Kingdom, as Egypt expanded into a genuine empire. Pharaohs Thutmose I and his grandson Thutmose III waged war against many of Egypt's neighbors, including the Nubians, the Canaanites, and the Mitanni. By the end of their reigns, Egypt stretched from modern-day Turkey all the way south to modern-day Ethiopia.

But that turned out to be the peak for Egypt. By making war with the other big Middle Eastern powers,

Egypt made strong enemies, and spent the next thousand years being invaded by, well, literally everyone. If you've been loyal to a sports team that struggles year after year . . . well, check out this historic losing streak.

YEAR	INVADER	WINNER
945 BC	Libyans	Libyans
730 BC	Nubians	Nubians
670 BC	Assyrians	Assyrians
568 BC	Babylonians	Babylonians
525 BC	Persians	Persians
332 BC	Macedonians	Macedonians
30 BC	Romans	Romans

MO' HONEY, MO' PROBLEMS

The 332 BC invasion of Egypt was led by Alexander the Great, who quickly had himself crowned pharaoh at the Temple of Ptah in Memphis. He then headed east to battle the Assyrians, Babylonians, and Persians. By 330 BC he was the king of Greece, pharaoh of Egypt, *and* king of Persia and Asia, all at the same time. Alexander ruled three different continents!

When Alexander died in Babylon of a fever, his body was placed in a gold sarcophagus filled with honey and was returned to Egypt, where it spent the next few centuries. But even after death he had a tough time of it. First, one of the last Egyptian pharaohs melted down the gold casket to make coins, and replaced the casket with a glass one. So now Alexander was basically floating in a glass jar full of honey. Then visiting Roman emperors kept bothering his body. Caligula stole his breastplate, and Caesar Augustus was said to have accidentally knocked off his nose!

MEGABOOKS

A booming new capital of Egypt was named for Alexander—and it still is today, the city of Alexandria. The Greeks founded Alexandria's most famous building—a library. The library at Alexandria soon became the greatest center of learning in the ancient world. They had a great method for building their collection.

A boat would arrive at the port of Alexandria.

$\rightarrow$

By law, any books aboard would be seized.

The sailors would get the copy of their book back.

$\leftarrow$ - - Scribes at the library would copy the whole book by hand.

The library kept the original!

You can't get a library card to the original Library of Alexandria—it burned down when Julius Caesar attacked Egypt in 48 BC. The library had hundreds of thousands of scrolls in its collection, so an unimaginable amount of knowledge just went up in smoke. Let's have a moment of silence, Junior Geniuses, for all the lost facts.

EXTRA CREDIT

In 2002 Egypt celebrated the new millennium by opening a rebuilt Library of Alexandria near the site of the ancient one. During the Egyptian Revolution of 2011, the people of Alexandria were determined that the new library wouldn't suffer the same fate as the old one. Hundreds of people joined hands to form a human chain around the library. Despite days of rioting, not a single pane of glass was broken.

END OF THE LINE

Alexander the Great's general Ptolemy Soter seized power in Egypt after Alexander died, and he began the last dynasty of Egypt, the Ptolemies. (The *P* is silent.) Three hundred years later, Ptolemy's descendant Cleopatra took the throne. She was forced to marry her own twelve-year-old brother and rule by his side, but they squabbled over the throne. You know how older sisters and little brothers are, even when they're not married!

Cleopatra headed to Rome to seek the help of Julius Caesar. According to the historian Plutarch, Cleopatra won Caesar's love by sneaking into his apartment hidden inside a rolled-up carpet.

After Caesar's death she fell in love with  his top general, Mark Antony, but their armies were defeated by Octavian at the Battle of Actium. Antony and Cleopatra both committed suicide, ending the three-thousand-year reign of the pharaohs over Egypt.

Egyptian culture still had a huge influence on the Mediterranean, of course. The famous columns on Greek temples were adapted from Egyptian architecture. Even their gods went overseas. The Greeks combined Thoth with their smartest god, Hermes, and the Romans began praying to Isis.

But soon Christianity began spreading through the Roman empire. The last Egyptian shrine to the old gods was the Temple of Isis on the Nile island of Philae. But in 535 AD the emperor Justinian closed the temple and converted it into a church.

One hundred years later Egypt was invaded by another Middle Eastern force, the Rashidun Caliphate.

Arabic became the national language, and Islam the new religion. The Arabs built a new capital at al-Qahira—or, as we know it today, Cairo.

TOMB RAIDERS

The mysteries of Egypt were mostly lost for centuries. One medieval author produced an Arabic manual

GRAVE-ROBBING FOR DUMMIES

for stealing riches from Egyptian tombs, called *The Book of Buried Pearls.* But for the most part, no one knew what lay in ruins under the desert sands, and no one really cared.

That all changed when Napoleon brought his army to Egypt in 1798 and became fascinated by pyramids and mummies. He called in a team of over 150 scientists to record his discoveries. Unfortunately, some of the early "Egyptologists" were more looters than scholars. A former circus strongman from Venice called "The Great Belzoni" pillaged literally tons of treasure, leaving a series of damaged tombs and temples in his wake.

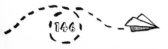

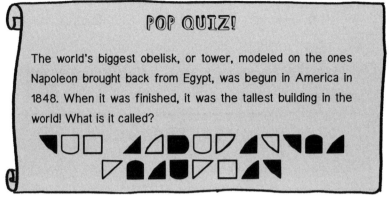

POP QUIZ!

The world's biggest obelisk, or tower, modeled on the ones Napoleon brought back from Egypt, was begun in America in 1848. When it was finished, it was the tallest building in the world! What is it called?

One of Napoleon's soldiers brought home what may be the most important Egyptian artifact ever: the famous Rosetta stone. This slab of rock is carved

with an official decree for King Ptolemy V—but the cool part is that the same message is carved in three languages: Greek, Demotic (a late Egyptian form of writing), and hieroglyphs.

The secret of Egyptian hieroglyphs had been lost for more than a thousand years, but a boy named Jean-François Champollion vowed when he was just eleven years old that he would figure them out one day. Champollion was an early Junior Genius—by the time he was thirteen, he could already read ancient languages such as Hebrew, Syriac, and Aramaic!

After decades spent studying the Rosetta stone and other carvings, Champollion finally cracked the code, and became world famous. He had brought a dead language back to life.

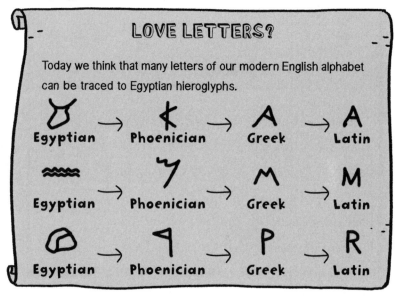

LOVE LETTERS?

Today we think that many letters of our modern English alphabet can be traced to Egyptian hieroglyphs.

Egyptian → Phoenician → Greek → Latin

Egyptian → Phoenician → Greek → Latin

Egyptian → Phoenician → Greek → Latin

BOY MEETS WORLD

Later, when the British occupied Egypt in the nineteenth century, more serious scholars started studying the ruins of ancient Egypt—and found that history was everywhere. The tomb of Queen Hetepheres was discovered by accident when a photographer's camera tripod abruptly sank into the sand. By chance it had fallen through the ceiling of the tomb!

In 1922, after five years of searching, Lord Carnarvon's expedition finally found and opened the tomb of the boy king Tutankhamen. The tomb contained more than five thousand priceless objects, so much stuff that it took Carnarvon's team, led by Howard Carter, eight years just to clear the tomb and another ten years to catalog its contents. Among the artifacts buried with "King Tut" were:

100 PAIRS OF SHOES

A FIRST AID KIT

30 BOOMERANGS

30 JARS OF WINE

139 WALKING STICKS

150 MAGIC AMULETS

DEATH ON THE NILE

On the same day Howard Carter opened Tutankhamen's tomb, a cobra slipped into his Luxor home and ate his prized pet canary! Then Lord Carnarvon died of blood poisoning a few months later. When a few other people connected with the Carnarvon family or the expedition died of illnesses in the years to come, the media became convinced that King Tut's tomb had been cursed!

Sorry, Junior Geniuses. In reality there was no warning of a "curse" inscribed anywhere on the tomb. Many members of the expedition lived long, happy lives, some into the 1960s. Carter himself didn't die until he got cancer at the age of sixty-four. **Beware the very slow-moving curse of the pharaohs!**

People were amazed by the treasures of King Tut's tomb, and the world caught "Egyptomania." Hollywood and almost a hundred other U.S. cities opened glamorous Egyptian theaters decorated with papyrus-shaped columns and hieroglyphics. Women put kohl around their eyes, put henna in their hair, and wore snake bracelets.

This modern fascination with ancient Egypt is still going strong today. There's a giant glass pyramid in front of the Louvre museum in Paris, and an even bigger one at the Luxor casino in Las Vegas. The Luxor even has a copy of the Great Sphinx that's bigger than the real one!

NOW AND THEN

If you ever get the chance to go to Egypt, you'll find that a lot has changed since the days of the pharaohs:

∘ The Temple of Ra at Heliopolis is now buried under a northern suburb of Cairo.

∘ The Great Sphinx at Giza doesn't stare off at a sandy horizon anymore. It's looking at a Pizza Hut and a KFC.

∘ The building of the Aswan High Dam put much of the Nile Valley underwater, so lower Nubia is now called "Lake Nasser." Luckily, the temples of Abu Simbel were saved from the flooding. They were cut into 1,042 sections and moved onto a high cliff above the dam. Other temples were shipped out of Egypt entirely. One was rebuilt in Madrid, Spain. Another can be seen at the Metropolitan Museum of Art in New York.

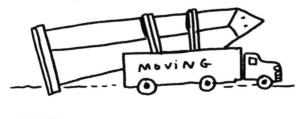

But some things haven't changed that much. Go out into rural Egypt, and homes will still be made of river mud, just like they were when Menes united Upper and Lower Egypt. Every year, two weeks before the start of Ramadan, a large boat parades through cheering crowds from the Mosque of Abu el-Haggag through the streets of Luxor—a reminder of the Opet fertility festival in ancient Thebes. And of course, five thousand people show up every day to marvel at the pyramids, now forty-five hundred years old and still going strong.

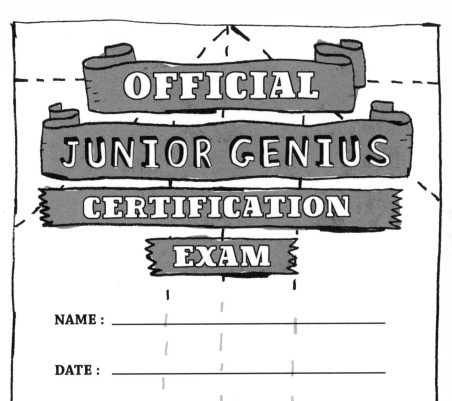

OFFICIAL
JUNIOR GENIUS
CERTIFICATION
EXAM

NAME : _____

DATE : _____

Here's the final test of your Egyptian knowledge, Junior Geniuses. Don't worry, I'm not going to weigh your heart on a scale like Anubis to see if you pass. All you have to do is answer the questions on the next few sheets of papyrus. Get a number 2 pencil and turn the page when I say "Begin."

Wait for it.

Wait for it. . . .

BEGIN.

1. Egyptian amulets called scarabs looked like what animals?

Ⓐ Cats   Ⓑ Cobras

Ⓒ Beetles   Ⓓ Vultures

2. Fill in the blank. The pharaoh Hatshepsut was remarkable for _____.

Ⓐ Worshipping only one god   Ⓑ Being a woman

Ⓒ Not speaking Egyptian   Ⓓ Building the biggest pyramids

3. What unusual hairstyle did Egyptian children all have?

Ⓐ Cornrows   Ⓑ A bowl cut

Ⓒ A sidelock   Ⓓ A "fauxhawk"

4. The mouth of the Nile River is a fan of waterways named for what letter of the Greek alphabet?

Ⓐ Alpha   Ⓑ Beta

Ⓒ Gamma   Ⓓ Delta

5. The world's biggest monolithic statue is found by the pyramids of Giza. What is it a statue of?

Ⓐ An obelisk   Ⓑ Amenhotep III

Ⓒ A sun god   Ⓓ A sphinx

6. What food has been found preserved and unspoiled in Egyptian tombs?

Ⓐ Honey   Ⓑ Barley

Ⓒ Onions   Ⓓ Dried fish

7. Which god avenged his father's death at the hands of Set?

Ⓐ Anubis   Ⓑ Atum

Ⓒ Horus   Ⓓ Thoth

8. When a pet cat died, Egyptian households mourned by doing what?

Ⓐ Shaving their eyebrows   Ⓑ Shaking a rattle

Ⓒ Sleeping in the temple   Ⓓ Wearing an ankh

9. What did the French scientist Jean-François Champollion study?

Ⓐ Mummies   Ⓑ Amulets

Ⓒ The Lighthouse of   Ⓓ Hieroglyphs
Alexandria

10. When a pharaoh began his thirtieth year on the throne, he had to prove his strength to Egypt by doing what?

Ⓐ Hunting a bull   Ⓑ Running a race

Ⓒ Fighting a war   Ⓓ Building a pyramid

11. The Egyptians invented the world's first artificial pigment. What color was it?

Ⓐ Blue   Ⓑ Black

Ⓒ Red   Ⓓ Green

12. What would you expect to find in a sarcophagus?

Ⓐ A ceremonial boat   Ⓑ Giant pillars

Ⓒ Mud and clay   Ⓓ A mummy

13. The Egyptian pharaoh nicknamed the "Striking Catfish" is best remembered today for what?

Ⓐ Defeating the Hyksos   Ⓑ Unifying Egypt

Ⓒ Marrying Cleopatra   Ⓓ Being delicious with grits

14. All night on his boat, Ra and his helmsman Set would battle what evil serpent?

Ⓐ Khepri   Ⓑ Osiris

Ⓒ Ammit   Ⓓ Apophis

15. What would an Egyptian write inside his cartouche?

Ⓐ His name   Ⓑ A calendar

Ⓒ A prayer to the gods   Ⓓ A map

THE OFFICIAL
JUNIOR GENIUS CIPHER

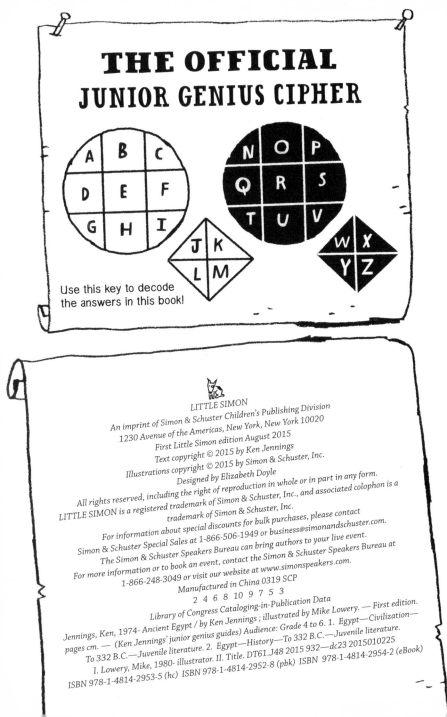

Use this key to decode
the answers in this book!

LITTLE SIMON

An imprint of Simon & Schuster Children's Publishing Division

1230 Avenue of the Americas, New York, New York 10020

First Little Simon edition August 2015

Text copyright © 2015 by Ken Jennings

Illustrations copyright © 2015 by Simon & Schuster, Inc.

Designed by Elizabeth Doyle

All rights reserved, including the right of reproduction in whole or in part in any form.
LITTLE SIMON is a registered trademark of Simon & Schuster, Inc., and associated colophon is a
trademark of Simon & Schuster, Inc.

For information about special discounts for bulk purchases, please contact
Simon & Schuster Special Sales at 1-866-506-1949 or business@simonandschuster.com.

The Simon & Schuster Speakers Bureau can bring authors to your live event.
For more information or to book an event, contact the Simon & Schuster Speakers Bureau at
1-866-248-3049 or visit our website at www.simonspeakers.com.

Manufactured in China 0319 SCP

2 4 6 8 10 9 7 5 3

Library of Congress Cataloging-in-Publication Data

Jennings, Ken, 1974- Ancient Egypt / by Ken Jennings ; illustrated by Mike Lowery. — First edition.
pages cm. — (Ken Jennings' junior genius guides) Audience: Grade 4 to 6. 1. Egypt—Civilization—
To 332 B.C.—Juvenile literature. 2. Egypt—History—To 332 B.C.—Juvenile literature.
I. Lowery, Mike, 1980- illustrator. II. Title. DT61.J48 2015 932—dc23 2015010225
ISBN 978-1-4814-2953-5 (hc) ISBN 978-1-4814-2952-8 (pbk) ISBN 978-1-4814-2954-2 (eBook)